D1760792

SCOTLAND
On This Day

FEBRUARY

WEDNESDAY 1st FEBRUARY 1984

Scotland captain Darren Fletcher was born on this day in Edinburgh. It took him some time to win acceptance, along with several medals, at Manchester United but eventually he became one of the finest midfielders in Europe. His development has, no doubt, been helped by exposure to international football at an early age. In only his second Scotland game, aged 19, he volleyed home a vital goal against Lithuania to fire his country to the Euro 2004 play-offs. Against Holland he set up James McFadden's goal with a marvellous back heel and early in the next year he became the youngest captain in over 100 years when he took the armband against Estonia aged 20. He has since firmly established himself as a first choice in midfield and was made captain on a permanent basis.

SUNDAY 1st FEBRUARY 2004

After a long battle with Alzheimer's disease, Ally MacLeod died aged 72. Scotland's manager in the 1978 World Cup shouldered a lot of the blame for the disaster in Argentina but the passing of time means most fans are happy to remember him for the fun – and the earlier victories – he brought to the game. In 2007 a group of fans walked from Ayrshire to Hampden for the Italy game in memory of Ally and to raise money for Alzheimer Scotland.

MONDAY 2nd FEBRUARY 1959

Those wishing to attend the under-23 match against England at Ibrox were let down by the weather as the match was postponed due to a frozen pitch. At least the guests were happy as the decision had been made two days before the Wednesday fixture to ensure they did not make a needless journey.

FRIDAY 3rd FEBRUARY 1950

While Alan Hansen is remembered as one of Scotland's finest defenders, it is often forgotten that his brother John, born in Sauchie on this day, was also an international defender. His impressive performances for Partick Thistle earned him two caps, against Belgium and Yugoslavia, while in between his international games he also collected a League Cup winner's medal when Thistle so memorably stunned Celtic in 1971.

SATURDAY 4TH FEBRUARY 1933

Jimmy Murray, who would score Scotland's first goal at the World Cup finals, was born in Edinburgh. Despite this notable accomplishment, his success with Scotland was limited in comparison to what he achieved with Hearts, and that strike against Yugoslavia was his only goal in five internationals.

WEDNESDAY 5TH FEBRUARY 1969

Billy Dodds was born in New Cumnock. The striker scored goals all over the country and he collected winner's medals in every major Scottish competition. He also picked up 26 Scotland caps, scoring seven goals. After playing he became a respected coach and popular pundit working in the media.

MONDAY 6TH FEBRUARY 1967

Scotland had appointed a couple of short-term managers after failing to reach the 1966 World Cup finals but hoped Bobby Brown, appointed on this day, would prove a lasting solution. He made the perfect start with victory over England at Wembley but struggled to replicate this success. After falling short in qualifying for the European Championships of 1968 and the World Cup of 1970, he made way for Tommy Docherty during the 1972 European campaign.

WEDNESDAY 6TH FEBRUARY 1991

Scotland faced the Soviet Union for the last time in 1991 when they went down 1-0 in a friendly at Ibrox. The countries had met four times in total with the Soviets winning three and drawing one – and that draw at the 1982 World Cup allowed them to progress while knocking out Scotland! Ironically, Scotland then defeated the Commonwealth of Independent States – the name used briefly after the collapse of the USSR – at Euro 92.

THURSDAY 7TH FEBRUARY 1963

Everton signed Scottish winger Alex Scott, paying Rangers £39,000. Several English clubs were interested in the player who had won every major honour in Scotland but his destination turned out to be Goodison Park. He enjoyed further success there, winning the championship and FA Cup, before returning to Scotland to end his career.

WEDNESDAY 8th FEBRUARY 1989

After a win and a draw in their opening qualifiers for the 1990 World Cup, Scotland maintained their momentum in dramatic fashion against Cyprus in Limassol. Seemingly weeks into injury time, although actually just at the beginning of the sixth minute, Richard Gough towered above the home defence to power home a sensational winner to earn Scotland the points. Cyprus had previously done enough to reach the 90-minute mark at 2-2 but were punished for their time-wasting throughout the second half. Mo Johnston and Gough had scored Scotland's earlier goals in what would prove to be a crucial win as rivals France only drew on the island.

SATURDAY 9th FEBRUARY 1957

Gordon Strachan was born in Edinburgh. While he started at Dundee, it was with Aberdeen he made his name as he played with the Pittodrie club during the greatest spell in their history. He collected league titles and cups aplenty with them, including the 1983 Cup Winners' Cup, and broke into the Scottish side before moving to Manchester United. In England he would win the FA Cup and then, with Leeds United, another championship while accumulating 50 caps for his country. He appeared at two World Cups, scoring in one, and then showed himself to be one of those rare beasts – a good player but also a good manager. He had worked mainly with smaller clubs in England but kept Coventry City in the Premiership and led Southampton to Europe via the FA Cup Final. At Celtic he won three championships in four seasons, along with a handful of domestic cups, and is widely considered a Scotland manager of the future.

FRIDAY 10th FEBRUARY 2006

Former Scotland manager John Prentice died on this day. He had earned his chance at the Scotland job after doing well in charge of Clyde and was employed by the SFA on a full-time basis while predecessor Jock Stein had split his attention with the Celtic job. Prentice led the team for only four games but despite a draw with world champions Brazil, he failed to win a match and returned to club management with Falkirk and Dundee. After football, he emmigrated to Australia.

GORDON STRACHAN COLLECTED 50 SCOTLAND CAPS AND WAS INDUCTED INTO THE HALL OF FAME.

TUESDAY 11TH FEBRUARY 1997

Scotland took on Estonia in the neutral venue of Monaco after a dispute over the kick-off time of the original fixture had seen the guests in Tallinn take to the field unopposed. Though the rules dictated Scotland should have been awarded a 3-0 win, Uefa decided otherwise. So it was that the Tartan Army found themselves mixing with the Monte Carlo jet set and drinking pints which were eye-wateringly expensive. Unsurprisingly, they were bitterly disappointed when Scotland produced a very poor performance and drew 0-0 with the Baltic side. Tempers frayed further when Ian Ferguson made offensive gestures to the fans as he walked off the pitch. Ferguson had endured a disappointing international career relative to his excellent club form for St Mirren and Rangers but that ended on this night as he was never given a chance to add to his nine caps.

WEDNESDAY 12TH FEBRUARY 2003

Berti Vogts may have believed that the Scottish side needed as much practice as possible but his insistence on playing at every opportunity was hard going for the fans. Despite a sizable support backing the Republic of Ireland, less than 34,000 were in attendance at Hampden to watch the visitors win 2-0 in what was a dismal game of football. In 2003, Vogts would be in charge for a remarkable 12 games of which six were friendly matches. During his entire spell as Scotland manager, there would be 18 friendly games and only 13 competitive contests. While Vogts organised the games with the best of intentions, his plans did not work as several players missed out on the warm-up games with minor niggles and injuries before being fit enough to play again for their clubs.

MONDAY 13TH FEBRUARY 1961

The Scotland under-23 side thrilled the crowd at Fir Park when they defeated the British Army 3-2 in a bounce game. A young Denis Law impressed with two goals in an exceptional display and local boy Ian St John – who would go on to gain 21 full international caps – scored the other. The army was far from defenceless though and one notable soldier in their line-up would go on to have a spectacular career in football – Jim Baxter.

WEDNESDAY 14TH FEBRUARY 1973

While the main celebrations for the centenary of the SFA would take place in summer, the festivities were kicked off with the annual Auld Enemy clash which took place in February. England were not gracious guests though as they arrived in Glasgow and turned in a thumping performance to win 5-0. The game was particularly unkind on goalkeeper Bobby Clark who had made an excellent start to his Scotland career, conceding less than a goal a game on average in his first 16 appearances. Judgement on goalkeepers has always been very harsh though and after this hammering, while earning his 17th Scotland cap, he was never picked again. He did have the consolation of winning the League Cup and Scottish championship with Aberdeen to go with his Scottish Cup winner's medal from 1970 before he decided to develop his post-playing career in football in America.

SATURDAY 15TH FEBRUARY 1896

Andrew Wilson, born on this day, was a rare sportsman who excelled enough at two competencies to be selected internationally for both. Along with playing football for Scotland, for whom he had the superb scoring record of 12 goals in 12 games, he also played bowls – but in that discipline he was picked for England!

MONDAY 15TH FEBRUARY 1954

The SFA council were informed that Andy Beattie had accepted the position offered to him as Scotland national team manager. For the first time the SFA were willing to relinquish some power in team matters but it would still be several years until the manager's job developed into something similar to current conditions when one person would be in near complete control of everything relating to the national squad.

TUESDAY 16TH FEBRUARY 1847

One of the most successful early footballers, Arthur Kinnaird, was born in London in 1847. He would win five FA Cup finals but as he was the son of a family from Perthshire, he would play his only international match for Scotland against England in 1873. Along with becoming the 11th Lord Kinnaird, he was also a notable administrator of the game in England.

WEDNESDAY 17TH FEBRUARY 1988

Scotland took on Saudi Arabia in a full international for the only time to date when they played out a 2-2 draw in Riyadh. Trailing 1-0 at half-time, goals from Mo Johnston and John Collins immediately turned the game around but the Saudis would find an equaliser of their own to ensure the honour was shared. Jim Leighton saw his record of 469 minutes without losing a goal end as he picked the ball out of the net for the first time since conceding against Belgium in April 1987.

WEDNESDAY 17TH FEBRUARY 1993

After a disappointing end to 1992, Scotland hoped 1993 would prove better. They started in positive fashion by ending a mini goal drought to defeat Malta 3-0 at Ibrox but after home draws against Portugal and Italy, the 1994 World Cup in America seemed farther away than just the distance across the Atlantic Ocean. The light relief in this game was provided by an Ally McCoist double and Pat Nevin, who added gloss to the victory with another goal late on.

MONDAY 18TH FEBRUARY 1974

The life of a footballer has many off-the-pitch obligations – meeting fans, talking to sponsors and giving media interviews all have to be undertaken with good grace. Quite what the World Cup squad of 1974 made of being told to convene in London to record Easy Easy four months before the tournament is unclear but with only a little cajoling they soon threw themselves into singing the official song for the summer with gusto.

WEDNESDAY 18TH FEBRUARY 2004

After losing the second leg of the Euro 2004 play-off 6-0 to Holland, Berti Vogts desperately needed a positive result to lift the fans in the next game. Being a goal down to Wales in Cardiff before a minute of football had been played was not part of the plan and neither was what followed – Wales, and hat-trick hero Robert Earnshaw in particular, tore apart the Scotland defence almost at will as they racked up a thumping 4-0 win. It was Wales' biggest-ever victory over Scotland.

SUNDAY 19TH FEBRUARY 1939

Future Scotland midfielder Paddy Crerand was born in Glasgow in 1939. Though he played for Celtic, he most commonly associated with Manchester United where he won several honours including the 1968 European Cup. As a tenacious competitor, he was sent off for Scotland in Bratislava in 1961, en route to being capped 16 times for his country.

SATURDAY 20TH FEBRUARY 1960

David Speedie was born on this day. He would play for Chelsea, Coventry City and Liverpool but fell just short of succeeding internationally. He made his debut in the Rous Cup win of 1985 and also played in the second leg of the 1985 play-off for Mexico against Australia but did not feature in the World Cups of 1986 or 1990. He finished his career with ten caps.

SATURDAY 21ST FEBRUARY 1931

Scotland were held to a draw in Belfast against Northern Ireland in their second game of the 1931 British Home Championship. The point was viewed with mixed feelings. Although it was an away draw which maintained Scotland's hopes of sharing the title with England, it also meant they could not win the championship outright. As the Irish lost to Wales and England perhaps the latter perspective was fairer.

TUESDAY 22ND FEBRUARY 1972

The future of Hampden Park was uncertain and eyebrows were raised when Glasgow City Council suggested a £750,000 renovation programme. There was a catch, however; the council would take ownership of the stadium.

WEDNESDAY 22ND FEBRUARY 1978

A crowd of nearly 60,000 turned up at Hampden to watch Scotland take on Bulgaria for the first time. With the British Home Championship providing the last games before the finals in Argentina, this was the only genuine friendly match the team would play in preparation. Archie Gemmill's penalty took Scotland into half-time with the score at 1-1 and Ian Wallace came off the bench to score the winner on his debut. It would be his only goal in three appearances.

SATURDAY 23rd FEBRUARY 1901

Scotland started the British Home Championship of 1901 in tremendous style by hammering Ireland 11-0 at Celtic Park. The hapless Irish were five goals down at half-time and by full time Scotland had achieved what remains – and will surely never be surpassed – their greatest-ever total. The goals were split mainly between Bob Hamilton of Rangers and Sandy McMahon of Celtic who grabbed four apiece. Hamilton, the captain on the day, had a distinguished international career which lasted from 1899 to 1911. He played 11 times for Scotland in this time, scoring 15 goals. Ironically, despite this huge win, Scotland would only draw against Wales and England in their later games and as England defeated Wales, the Scots would finish the tournament as only runners-up.

WEDNESDAY 23rd FEBRUARY 1927

Scotland manager Willie Ormond was born. He took over the national team in 1973 and a famous victory over Czechoslovakia took the side to the World Cup finals in 1974. In West Germany the side performed admirably but exited after the first round on goal difference. After a narrow failure in reaching the European Championships of 1976, the SFA decided a change was needed during the World Cup campaign of 1978 and Ormond left Hampden to take over at Hearts.

MONDAY 24th FEBRUARY 1948

A second Scotland manager was born on this day, Walter Smith. Smith enjoyed a rather modest playing career but as a coach and manager he was immensely successful. He was part of Jim McLean's backroom staff at Dundee United as they won the Premier League in 1983 and moved to Rangers as assistant-manager to Graeme Souness in 1986. Following the departure of Souness to Liverpool, he was made Rangers manager in 1991 and collected six titles and several cups before moving on to Everton, and then Manchester United as assistant to Sir Alex Ferguson. After the disastrous Vogts era he picked up the pieces for Scotland and restored some pride in the 2006 World Cup qualifying campaign before starting the Euro 2008 campaign with three victories, including a success over France. Rangers remained his greater love though and he returned to Ibrox as manager early in 2007.

SATURDAY 24TH FEBRUARY 1940

Scottish record scorer Denis Law was born in Aberdeen. Despite his birth north of the border, his football was played mainly in England, with a short sojourn in Italy at Torino. A prolific scorer, he was part of the great Manchester United side of the late 1960s but missed out on the European Cup triumph of 1968 with injury. His 30 Scotland goals in just 55 games remains a record shared with Kenny Dalglish, although the latter needed nearly twice as many appearances to reach the same tally.

WEDNESDAY 24TH FEBRUARY 1982

Scotland's preparation for the World Cup of 1982 began with a friendly against hosts Spain in Valencia. The Scots would play their group matches in the tournament in Malaga and Seville and may have been pleased at not having to return to the Luis Casanova Stadium – later Mestalla – as they lost convincingly, 3-0.

SATURDAY 25TH FEBRUARY 1956

Davie Cooper was born on this day. Though a talented footballer, he seemed set to drift out of the game until tempted to Clydebank in 1974. He lit up Kilbowie and earned a move to Rangers, where he won several honours and started his international career. He was blessed with tremendous skill and made a big contribution to the Scotland cause by scoring a crucial pair of goals against Wales and Australia on the road to the World Cup finals in Mexico. He should probably have been capped more than 22 times. A recall to the squad for the last qualifying game for Italia 90 seemed set to take him to his second World Cup but injury ruled him out of the finals.

WEDNESDAY 25TH FEBRUARY 1981

Political difficulties caused Israel to be included in the European qualifying section of the 1982 World Cup and Scotland faced the side for the first time in a Tel Aviv clash of 1981. Kenny Dalglish scored the only goal of the game in what proved an important victory en route to qualification as every other country in the group dropped points when visiting the Israelis.

THURSDAY 26TH FEBRUARY 1931

Scotland manager Ally MacLeod was born in Glasgow. He started his long career in football by signing for Third Lanark while still at school and had a debut to remember – though not in the traditional sense. During the game against Stirling Albion, the stand at Cathkin Park caught fire and at full time the players had to dash quickly to grab clothes and belongings before making a sharp exit! The highlight of his playing career was an FA Cup Final with Blackburn Rovers but he soon made his mark as a manager at Ayr United and Aberdeen which earned him the Scotland job in 1977. He never seemed quite recovered from the huge highs, and then massive lows, of that position but continued in football for more than ten years after the 1978 World Cup, managing Ayr United (twice), Motherwell, Airdrie and Queen of the South before retiring.

THURSDAY 26TH FEBRUARY 1981

Michael Stewart was born in 1981. The midfielder played three times for his country under Berti Vogts but then had to wait more than six years to gain his fourth, and to date, final cap when he faced Northern Ireland under the management of George Burley. Stewart's well-travelled career saw him start at Manchester United but he had a spell on loan at their feeder club in Belgium, Royal Antwerp, along with Nottingham Forest. He then went to Edinburgh where he criss-crossed the city to play for Hearts, Hibs and then Hearts again before moving to Gençlerbirliği in the Turkish capital of Ankara to start the next chapter of his nomadic football career.

WEDNESDAY 27TH FEBRUARY 1985

Scotland made a poor start to 1985 which threatened to cost them a place at the World Cup finals in Mexico in 1986. After opening the campaign with two victories, they lost 1-0 on this day to Spain in Seville and would then suffer another defeat at home to Wales a month later. That meant winning the group and qualifying automatically was almost certainly impossible and instead there would be a tough battle with Wales, involving a crunch match in Cardiff, to secure the play-off spot against the winner of the Oceanic qualifying group.

FRIDAY 28TH FEBRUARY 1930

After failing to qualify for the World Cup on multiple occasions, the SFA could be forgiven for wishing for a return to the old days when all that was needed to enter the finals was an application form and a stamp. The first World Cup, held in Uruguay in 1930, was open to all Fifa members with a deadline for entry at the end of February. However, at the deadline no European countries had indicated a willingness to make the long journey to South America and it required the personal intervention of Fifa president Jules Rimet who ensured the eventual participation of Belgium, France, Yugoslavia and Romania. The Yugoslavs were the most successful representatives of the continent as they reached the semi-finals but were crushed 6-1 by the hosts.

MONDAY 28TH FEBRUARY 1972

The SFA accepted an invitation from Brazil to play in the Independence Cup, a mini-World Cup tournament which would take place in the summer. Scotland would skip the opening stages and join the competition in the second round which saw eight countries split into two groups. As well as facing hosts Brazil, Scotland would also be up against qualifiers Yugoslavia and another invited nation, Czechoslovakia.

WEDNESDAY 29TH FEBRUARY 1956

Injury and withdrawals severely hampered the Scotland B team which took on their English equivalents at Dens Park on this day. They were eventually unlucky to take only a draw from the encounter. No players who had made more than one appearance in the British Home Championship were considered but many of the up-and-coming youngsters who were supposed to benefit from this game were unable to feature. That meant many replacements were called up who knew that they had no realistic chance of forcing themselves into contention for the A squad but they produced a determined performance nonetheless. Willie McCulloch and Jimmy Mulkerrin had put Scotland 2-1 up in front of a crowd of over 11,000 before England levelled with only two minutes still to play. Neither of the Scottish scorers would go on to be capped for the full national side.

SCOTLAND
On This Day

MARCH

SATURDAY 1st MARCH 1924

One of the most prolific strikers of the Scottish national team was Hughie Gallacher, who made his debut in the British Home Championship victory over Northern Ireland on this day. Though he failed to find the net in this particular clash, he did bag a double while earning his next cap against Wales and finished his Scotland career with the remarkable tally of 23 goals from 20 games, a record which puts him behind only Denis Law and Kenny Dalglish in the all-time scoring chart. Hughie played in the Wembley Wizards team of 1928 but did not score on that occasion.

SUNDAY 1st MARCH 1959

Andy Beattie took charge of the Scotland international side for the second time when he replaced Matt Busby. Having resigned in protest over squad issues at the 1954 World Cup, he returned to lead Scotland to a modest share of the British Home Championship in 1959/60, courtesy of an away win over Northern Ireland, and draws at home to both England and Wales. With England and Wales also defeating the Irish and drawing against each other, the title was split three ways. He did record notable friendly wins at home to West Germany, and in Holland, but resigned once more in November 1960 citing his commitments to Nottingham Forest.

MONDAY 1st MARCH 1999

Tommy Pearson, the only player to feature on both sides of the Auld Enemy clash, died in 1999. Based in the north-east of England as a player with Newcastle United, he was in the crowd anticipating a wartime international when news emerged that hosts England would be a man short due to a traffic accident involving one of their players. Tommy stepped in to fill the void but may have had mixed feelings in contributing to a 2-1 victory for the English! A few years later he made his official international debut, but for Scotland, against England in a 1-1 draw at Hampden before making a final appearance a month later in a loss to Belgium in Brussels. After football Tommy continued his sporting endeavour in the form of golf and was an excellent amateur player, even competing in the Open Championship.

SATURDAY 2ND MARCH 1878

Scotland taught England a football lesson in Glasgow with a thumping 7-2 win. Along with the high margin of victory, the match was notable for John McDougall scoring the first Scotland hat-trick while McGregor, McKinnon and McNeil with a double, also made the score-sheet. McDougall was a very successful player domestically as he helped Vale of Leven to win three successive Scottish Cups in the 1870s but there were few internationals to play and he ended his career with four goals and five caps. After football he went on to become a successful businessman.

THURSDAY 2ND MARCH 1967

New manager Bobby Brown led a side to England for the first time when the under-23 team played in Newcastle. Despite conceding a goal to a soft penalty kick, the side were on a run of good form and triumphed 3-1. It would not be the last success south of the border in 1967!

SATURDAY 2ND MARCH 2002

Berti Vogts settled into his first full day in charge of the national team but the German would not have a particularly successful spell as Scotland boss. The early omens were not good. In his first game Scotland crashed to a 5-0 friendly thrashing in Paris against France before he endured the embarrassment of needing a second-half comeback to secure a 2-2 draw in the Faroe Islands in his competitive debut. Despite this poor start, Vogts managed to guide the side to the runners-up spot in the qualifying group for the 2004 European Championships but more humiliation lay in wait as the team were demolished 6-1 on aggregate by Holland in the play-offs. Vogts oversaw several other woeful results in friendly matches, including a 4-0 loss in Wales and a 3-0 humbling at home to Hungary, before collecting a mere two points from the first three matches of the next qualifying campaign saw him sacked from his post.

WEDNESDAY 3RD MARCH 1954

Which was the first Scotland side to play under floodlights? The B team of 1954 who secured a 1-1 draw against England at Roker Park, Sunderland.

SUNDAY 4TH MARCH 1951

When Kenneth Mathieson Dalglish was born on this day in Dalmarnock, Glasgow, no one could have imagined just what impact he would have on football – not just in Scotland but in England and far beyond too. Major honours simply flowed into his trophy cabinet after he became a mainstay of the Celtic side which was still in a period of dominance which would bring them nine championships in a row. Kenny collected four in total in Glasgow, along with four Scottish Cups and a League Cup, before moving to Liverpool for a British record transfer fee where, astonishingly, things were even better. At Anfield he became a hero of the Kop as he claimed seven championships and three European Cups along with several other domestic pots and established himself as arguably the best striker in Europe. His international career also flourished as he became the only Scottish player to rack up 100 caps, ending on 102 appearances, and he matched the scoring record of 30 goals set by Denis Law. Notable strikes came at the World Cup finals of 1978 and 1982 while he also scored an iconic header in the clash with Wales which ensured the side would be making the long journey to Argentina. The strike which matched Law's tally was also one to remember, a drive high into the roof of the Spanish goal in a famous Hampden victory, though many fans will recall just as fondly his 'rocket' which deceived Ray Clemence and found the net through the legs of the English goalkeeper in 1976. The Dalglish magic was not just confined to the pitch as he also led Liverpool to the club's first-ever league and cup double as a player-manager with other successes to follow. After suddenly resigning in 1991, he had a period out of football before returning to management with Blackburn Rovers where, with Jack Walker's backing, he took the club back into the top flight of English football and even to the championship in 1995. Further posts followed at Newcastle United and Celtic before a long pause from the game and a 2009 return to Liverpool and a role in the youth academy, and a position as club ambassador. He was named as part of Scotland's greatest team in a 2010 television series but even without such a contrived honour, he will always be cherished as one of the very best forwards ever produced by this country.

MONDAY 5TH MARCH 1877

It took several years of international football before Scotland benefitted from an own goal but it is not clear which Welshman holds the unfortunate honour of being the first to make this contribution. Some sources say it was 'Powell' but he does not appear to be listed in the Welsh team for this match. Regardless, Scotland were already heading for victory in Wrexham thanks to a second-half goal from captain Charles Campbell before the late 'oggie' made things safe.

MONDAY 6TH MARCH 1911

Ninian Park in Cardiff hosted its first international fixture in 1911 when Scotland visited for a British Home Championship match. A crowd of 14,000 was in attendance as Wales looked to inaugurate their new ground with a win but the majority of onlookers were to be left disappointed. Wales seemed to have done enough to secure the points but Robert Hamilton's last-minute equaliser, his second goal of the game, ensured a share of the spoils. Scotland would make many more trips to Cardiff and Ninian Park over the years but the ground is probably best known for being the venue for the match against Wales in 1985 which ended with the death of Jock Stein. A commemorative plaque took pride of place at Ninian Park until the stadium was knocked down in 2009 and Cardiff City moved to a new home across the road. Appropriately enough, the first international at the new stadium also saw Scotland take on Wales later that year although on this occasion the hosts were superior as they easily triumphed 3-0.

TUESDAY 6TH MARCH 1923

An application to the Glasgow Magistrates' Committee to hold a flag day in protest at the SFA fixing a 2s (10p) minimum admission price for a forthcoming international match was turned down. The plan was for those who purchased a flag to pledge themselves to abstain from going to the match, with any further money raised being donated to the Lord Provost's Relief fund. The protestors had hoped to force the SFA into halving the price of admission but despite the complaints, 25,000 watched the next home game against Wales in Paisley and over 70,000 entered Hampden Park for the later visit of England.

SATURDAY 7TH MARCH 1908

Scotland made a winning start to the British Home Championship of 1908 when Wales were defeated in Dundee. Dens Park was the venue as goals from Alec Bennett and William Lennie helped to secure a 2-1 victory. Scotland would go on to enjoy a successful campaign with a further win over Ireland and a draw against England ensuring a share of the championship with the latter.

SATURDAY 8TH MARCH 1873

After the first official international between Scotland and England produced a goalless draw in Glasgow in 1872, it would take until the rematch the next year for the Scots to register their first recognised goal. That honour fell to Henry Renny-Tailyour of Royal Engineers who scored the first of Scotland's two goals but he could not prevent the team slumping to a 4-2 defeat. The other Scottish marksman on the day was Clydesdale's William Gibb.

WEDNESDAY 8TH MARCH 1967

Bobby Brown announced that 17 of the 18 man squad which would take part in a world tour later in the year had been decided. The final place was not yet confirmed as personal circumstances could yet stop the player in question from travelling. The tour was made up by a Scotland XI, rather than the official team, meaning the matches were not officially recognised but it was still believed to be a worthwhile exercise to give younger players a taste of playing international football as part of early preparations for the 1970 World Cup. The manager's choices were restricted by Aberdeen, Hibs, Dundee United, Dundee, Chelsea, Sunderland, Manchester United, Liverpool and Spurs all going on their own tours and taking their players with them while further problems were also caused by the potential of Celtic and Rangers to reach the finals of their respective European competitions. Despite the restrictions placed on the manager, the tour was still a success with nine games bringing nine victories, including three over Australia in Sydney, Adelaide and Melbourne. The tour kicked off with a win over Israel in Tel Aviv and concluded nearly a month later with a win over Canada in Winnipeg. One can only imagine the reaction if the SFA announced a similar end-of-season tour these days!

SATURDAY 9TH MARCH 1889

One of Scotland's biggest-ever wins came on this day. Ibrox Park was the venue but the vast stadium was almost empty as only 5,000 spectators were in attendance. Those who turned up were treated to a scintillating Scottish performance against Ireland as a hat-trick by William Groves led the way to a 7-0 victory.

SATURDAY 10TH MARCH 1888

Easter Road in Edinburgh, home of Hibs, hosted an international for the first time in 1888. A crowd of 8,000 turned up to watch Scotland stroll to victory against Wales as they easily came out on top 5-1.

SUNDAY 11TH MARCH 1956

The Federation of Senior Supporters' Associations was anxious that their members received a greater allocation of tickets for big matches such as Scotland against England. The body decided at its AGM to rely on the press continuing to draw attention to their claim.

FRIDAY 11TH MARCH 1977

Archie Gemmill was released from hospital after a 24-hour stay following surgery. This was follow-up treatment after the unfortunate Gemmill had suffered a triple head fracture, an incident which had taken place not on international duty but during training with Derby County. In 1970, Gemmill had driven his pregnant wife from Derby to Paisley to ensure the birth of his child would take place north of the border and just to remove any final doubt about his patriotism, named his son, who would also play internationally, Scotland – though he is commonly known as Scot.

MONDAY 12TH MARCH 1973

Willie Ormond had problems ahead of the forthcoming under-23 clash against Wales in Swansea. Alan Rough of Partick Thistle, Eddie Kelly of Arsenal and Derek Johnstone of Rangers all pulled out while the press also made a big deal of the manager's decision to call up Andy McCulloch of Cardiff. Though the manager had not seen him play he was a prolific scorer but the story had a little twist as he was actually born in England.

THURSDAY 13TH MARCH 1873

The Scottish Football Association was formed by eight clubs in 1873. Queen's Park, Clydesdale, Vale of Leven, Dumbreck, Third Lanark, Eastern, Granville and Kilmarnock were the original members who created the body which retains overall responsibility for the game in Scotland to this day, ranging from amateurs playing in public parks to the national team entering major tournaments.

SATURDAY 13TH MARCH 1982

Colin Calderwood made his professional debut for Mansfield Town shortly after his 17th birthday but his football career began in very auspicious circumstances. An error had been made somewhere along the line with his registration and as it turned out he was ineligible to play. The club were docked two points for fielding him! Thankfully for Colin this setback had no lasting impact on his career and he later featured for Spurs, Aston Villa and Nottingham Forest on his way to winning 36 Scotland caps and appearing at Euro 96 in England and the World Cup finals in 1998. His only international goal came against San Marino.

MONDAY 13TH MARCH 2006

Scotland and Celtic legend Jimmy 'Jinky' Johnstone died on this day after a long battle with motor neurone disease. Johnstone was one of Scotland's most talented players and, combined with his feisty nature on the pitch and habit for getting into compromising situations off it, he will never be forgotten. His final number of caps was only 23 as he often lost out to Willie Henderson, his rival from Rangers, when it came to being selected for the national side. Despite being part of the squad at the 1974 World Cup he never took to the field in West Germany although he did earn further caps after the tournament. His most infamous incident occurred after a team-bonding session in Largs before the party left for the World Cup as over-exuberance saw him jettisoned in a rowing boat, minus the oars, and pushed off into the water! The players involved in the jape were not overly popular as the coastguard was eventually required to perform a rescue. Johnstone ended his career having won every domestic honour and the European Cup while his contribution to Scottish football will be long remembered.

TUESDAY 14TH MARCH 1916

Dawson Walker, the manager who led Scotland to their first point in the World Cup finals, was born. Walker was handed control of the national team on a temporary basis due to the Munich air crash of 1958 which left Matt Busby unable to take the side to Sweden. Dawson saw his men score for the first time at the finals as they drew 1-1 with Yugoslavia but narrow losses to Paraguay and France (3-2 and 2-1, respectively) saw the team finish bottom of the group and leave Sweden after falling at the first hurdle.

SATURDAY 15TH MARCH 1902

Wales continued their tour of Scottish football grounds when they were sent to Greenock for a British Home Championship clash. This time Cappielow, home of Greenock Morton, was blessed with its only full international fixture as Scotland easily swept aside the Welsh with a comprehensive 5-1 victory. Alec Smith was the hero for Scotland as he scored a hat-trick while Albert Buick and Jock Drummond added the other goals which helped secure the points.

THURSDAY 15TH MARCH 2007

It was announced that SFA chief executive David Taylor would leave his post at the end of the month. However, unlike his predecessor Jim Farry, Taylor was not forced to leave office because of a scandal but rather due to moving onwards and upwards in the world. Uefa had appointed him general secretary, the new title the body was giving to the job previously known as chief executive, and for several years a Scot held one of the most powerful positions in the governing body of European football. Taylor had been considered a success in his role with the SFA but he inevitably also received criticism for his part in the disastrous appointment of Berti Vogts as national team manager. Some fans also questioned the timing of the move as Taylor had, just over two months before news of his own departure broke, voiced the association's disappointment that Walter Smith was stepping away from the job of national manager to return to Rangers. Taylor's time as general secretary of Uefa ended in 2007 when he was replaced by his deputy, Gianni Infantino, from Italy.

MONDAY 16TH MARCH 1959

Scotland took on the Scottish League under the floodlights of Ibrox as a warm-up in preparation for the clash with England in April. The players produced a thrilling game as the Scottish League triumphed 6-5 with the league side boasting several promising young players who were hoping to go on to earn full international recognition. Bert McCann of Motherwell's Ancell Babes would go on to win five Scottish caps while John White – who was the best player on the pitch in this game – would collect 22, scoring three goals in the process.

SATURDAY 17TH MARCH 1888

Scotland's heavy 5-0 loss at home to England in 1888 shattered a number of impressive records. It was the first-ever Scottish defeat on home soil, the first English win north of the border and the first Scottish loss of any kind in nine years and 19 games. Furthermore, it was the first time Scotland failed to score in a match for 16 years, dating all the way back to the very first international between the countries in 1872. Proving that if you are going to blow a record you might as well do so properly, Scotland were four goals down by half-time in what was a disastrous outing. There were few positives to take from the match but a minor consolation was that John Goodall, one of England's best players, had been raised in Kilmarnock after his London birth.

SATURDAY 17TH MARCH 1906

The British Home Championship of 1906 was shared between Scotland and England. Scotland reached a notable landmark en route as Thomas Fitchie scored the 300th international goal for the country when Ireland were defeated 1-0 in Dublin. Not only was this a historic strike, it was also an important goal in an important win as it set up Scotland for a do or die clash against England at Hampden in the last match of the tournament. England needed only a draw for outright victory in the competition but goals either side of half-time from James Howie put Scotland in command as they looked to share the Home Championship with the English. The visitors pulled one back late on but it was not enough.

WEDNESDAY 18TH MARCH 1931

Footballers are not always renowned for their ingenuity in coming up with nicknames but Ian McMillan – dubbed the Wee Prime Minister – fared better than most. Born on this day, he earned the moniker through a combination of his authoritative style of play and the Prime Minister of the day being Harold Macmillan. The inside-forward earned six full caps for Scotland and scored his only goals in the form of a double in a convincing 6-0 win over the United States.

SATURDAY 19TH MARCH 1898

Motherwell had recently moved to their new Fir Park ground and the SFA offered them some support in the form of the Wales international in 1898. The club board carried out extensive work to raise the capacity to 15,000 but only 7,000 – then a record crowd for the ground – watched Scotland win 5-2. Fir Park would become a regular venue for youth internationals but this match remains the only occasion the full side have ever played a game in Motherwell.

SATURDAY 19TH MARCH 1910

Scotland had little to celebrate on the day of their 100th international when they lost 1-0 to Ireland in Belfast. A quick recovery and win against England at Hampden two weeks later did ensure the Home Championship was clinched outright for the last time in several years. The outbreak of the First World War caused the tournament to be cancelled and Scotland would not be able to call themselves champions of the islands again until 1921, though they did share the title with England in 1912.

MONDAY 19TH MARCH 1923

Future Scotland player and manager Bobby Brown was born in Dunipace. He turned professional with Rangers in 1946 though he remained a part-time player during his spell at Ibrox as he also taught PE at Denny High School. The goalkeeper was capped three times but his contribution to the national team is better remembered following his appointment as manager in 1967. His first senior game was the famous 3-2 victory over England at Wembley but further success proved elusive and he left in 1971.

SATURDAY 20TH MARCH 1886

John Lambie, of Queen's Park, is the youngest-ever Scottish player and scorer. He was aged just 17 years, three months and two days when he netted Scotland's fourth in a 7-2 rout of Ireland in Belfast.

SATURDAY 21ST MARCH 1896

International football arrived in Dundee before Dens Park was even built. Scotland played Wales in the city's first international match in 1896 at Carolina Port, the early home of Dundee FC, but the venue was hemmed in by the docks and unsuitable for expansion so the club left in 1899. The Welsh may have been glad they never had to return – they lost 4-0.

WEDNESDAY 22ND MARCH 1995

The nation was sent into shock with the news that Davie Cooper had suffered a brain haemorrhage while filming a coaching session with children. Despite being rushed to hospital he died the next day, aged 39. Spontaneous tributes emerged at Ibrox and Fir Park while fans of the national team were able to reflect on his two goals in 1985 which helped take the side to the Mexico World Cup. Cooper was blessed with a superb left foot and was undoubtedly one of the most talented players of his generation. He was unfortunate that his best years were spent in a struggling Rangers side and he lacked the extra pace which would have taken his game to an even higher level.

TUESDAY 23RD MARCH 1982

Scotland qualified for the under-18 European Championship later by drawing 2-2 with England in Coventry after winning the first leg 1-0. The youngsters were in trouble when they trailed 2-0 in the tie but a superb comeback, inspired by Paul McStay, set them on the path to glory later in the summer.

WEDNESDAY 23RD MARCH 2005

The world rankings were often derided as being unfair and meaningless but there was still a gnashing of teeth when it emerged Scotland had sunk to position 88 – their lowest in history – early in 2005.

MONDAY 24th MARCH 1947

Archie Gemmill, the scorer of one of Scotland's most famous goals, was born on this day in Paisley. Gemmill was both a solid competitor and talented player who could produce some inspired moments of skill at crucial times. That was epitomised by his wonderful solo goal against Holland in the 1978 World Cup which put Scotland 3-1 up and, albeit only briefly, into dreamland – and just one more goal from the next round. Being forever associated with such a moment does have a slight downside though as it is easy to forget the three English championships and European Cup that he won with Derby County and Nottingham Forest, while in total he played 43 times for Scotland, scoring eight goals.

SATURDAY 24th MARCH 2007

Scotland needed a scrambled last-minute goal from Craig Beattie to defeat Georgia 2-1 at Hampden and keep alive hope of reaching the European Championships in 2008. This game also returned the title of Unofficial World Champions to Scotland, a system based on the boxing method of becoming champion by defeating the existing title holder. Scotland and England, having played the first internationals, shared the vast majority of early victories between them in 'title bouts' with Scotland still holding the record for the longest time as world champions.

SATURDAY 25th MARCH 1876

Wales entered the international arena when they travelled to Glasgow to face Scotland in 1876 but were defeated 4-0. A quirk in the Scottish line-up was that brothers – Harold and Moses McNeil – played together for the first time. This was the single occasion the McNeils were in the same team as Moses collected only one more cap when Harold did not play. Harold finished his career with ten caps and six goals.

FRIDAY 25th MARCH 1966

John Prentice took over as manager as the team looked to bounce back from failing to qualify for the 1966 World Cup in England. He was in charge for only four games and drew against Brazil but losses to England, Holland and Portugal saw him leave the post later in the year.

WEDNESDAY 26TH MARCH 1986

Kenny Dalglish became the first, and to date only, player to reach the 100 cap mark for Scotland with this appearance against Romania in a Hampden friendly. The hosts cruised to victory but with the goals coming from Gordon Strachan, Richard Gough and Roy Aitken, Dalglish failed to find the net himself. The achievement in reaching 100 caps can be put in perspective by looking at the players with the second and third highest number of appearances. Jim Leighton, with 91, is a goalkeeper, while the closest outfield player is Alex McLeish, who trails some way behind with 77.

TUESDAY 27TH MARCH 1951

One of the briefest Scotland careers on record belongs to Ronnie Glaven and he was born on this day in 1951. After making his mark with Partick Thistle, who he helped win the League Cup in 1971, he successfully made the step across town to join Celtic. His career continued to blossom and he received international recognition in the friendly victory against Sweden in 1977. Unfortunately for Ronnie, he collected an injury after a mere three minutes of play and had to be substituted. The injury was a double blow as he was not recalled to the squad and he missed out of the Scottish Cup Final two weeks later which Celtic won 1-0 against Rangers!

WEDNESDAY 28TH MARCH 1990

Scotland's preparations for the 1990 World Cup continued with a match at home to world champions Argentina in Glasgow. Though Diego Maradona was not playing, eyebrows would have been raised around the globe as a fantastic strike from Stewart McKimmie – his only goal for Scotland – earned the hosts a famous 1-0 victory.

WEDNESDAY 28TH MARCH 2001

Veteran captain Colin Hendry became the oldest player to score for Scotland, aged 35 years, three months and 21 days, when he broke the deadlock in a World Cup qualifier against San Marino at Hampden Park. He actually scored a double but thoughts of celebrations were dampened with a late red card for lashing out at an opponent and the subsequent lengthy ban effectively ended his international career.

SATURDAY 29TH MARCH 1894

Scotland claimed the first-ever British Home Championship with a home win over Wales in Glasgow. A point would have sufficed to take the title but the side delivered the glory in style with a 4-1 triumph. Scotland would win the Home Championship outright a further 23 times and have a share in a further 17 triumphs.

SATURDAY 29TH MARCH 1997

Rugby Park in Kilmarnock was used for a full international for the final time when Estonia visited in spring 1997. Hampden's redevelopment forced the SFA to take matches around the country and the ground was crammed to the rafters for this vital World Cup qualifier. Tommy Boyd's only international goal for Scotland helped secure a precious 2-0 win en route to France 98.

WEDNESDAY 30TH MARCH 1983

Charlie Nicholas capped his international debut with a sensational equaliser against Switzerland in a European Championship qualifier at Hampden Park. Scotland were heading for defeat as they trailed by two goals when John Wark pulled one back late in the second half. Suddenly inspired, the Scotland players increased their efforts and Nicholas bagged a brilliant goal when he controlled a hopeful flick on his right foot by pulling the ball back to his left for a volley into the far corner. Scotland failed to qualify for the finals but the fightback and the equalising goal in particular will live long in the memory.

SATURDAY 31ST MARCH 1928

Scotland produced a sensational performance to hammer England 5-1 at Wembley and move into the history books. The side dubbed as the Wembley Wizards ran riot against their English counterparts and though they were already two goals up at half-time thanks to Alex Jackson and Alex James, it was in the second half that they made their quality show. The Scottish passing game left the lumbering England side chasing shadows across the soaking Wembley pitch and, while Jackson completed his hat-trick and James added another before Bob Kelly claimed a consolation, the final margin of victory could easily have been much higher than it was at the final whistle.

SCOTLAND
On This Day

APRIL

SATURDAY 1st APRIL 1933

An era ended on this day as the last amateurs to play for the full Scotland team took to the field against England in a British Home Championship tie. James Crawford of Queen's Park was one while the other, his teammate Bob Gillespie, even had the honour of being the last amateur captain. They ended on a high as two goals from Jimmy McGrory secured a 2-1 victory. After retiring from playing, Gillespie remained involved with Queen's Park and put his skills as a chartered accountant to good effect by being secretary and treasurer for the club.

SATURDAY 1st APRIL 1978

If a modern Scotland World Cup song boasted that the country was going to win the tournament it would be safe to assume tongues would be firmly planted in cheeks. This was definitely not the case in 1978 when Andy Cameron's hit Ally's Tartan Army peaked in the charts at number six. This classic Scotland tune is still heard in the pre-match build-up and though everyone may have been left looking silly afterwards, the song played its part in anticipating the big day when the squad would leave for Argentina.

SATURDAY 2nd APRIL 1927

Scotland's longest run without conceding a goal came to an end in this home defeat to England. The visitors scored in the 69th minute of the clash en route to a 2-1 victory and this was the first goal Scotland had lost since conceding a 43rd-minute strike to Wales in February 1925. Together with the seven complete clean sheets kept between the goals and the extra minutes from the games at either end of the run, the record stands, to this day, at 742 minutes – over 12 hours of football!

SATURDAY 2nd APRIL 1955

How many positives can be taken from a 7-2 defeat against England at Wembley? Not many but one was Tommy Docherty netting Scotland's 600th goal of all time as he scored a consolation free kick late on. It salvaged only a modicum of pride as Scotland slumped to their heaviest defeat against England to date.

SATURDAY 3RD APRIL 1954

Fifa had once more allowed the British Home Championship to act as a qualifying group for the World Cup and on this occasion Scotland wisely decided to accept their place at the tournament even if they finished runners-up. That was a good choice because in this decider for the Home Championship at Hampden they needed to win to overtake England and claim first place but were instead well beaten, 4-2. Allan Brown actually opened the scoring for the Scots but England fought back in style and by the time the second Scottish goal arrived in the final minute, the match had been well and truly lost.

SATURDAY 4TH APRIL 1903

The record for the longest-spanning Scotland career belongs to Edward Doig who collected five caps over a period of 16 years, one month and 17 days. Ned had made his debut in a win against Ireland in 1887 and played in another win over the Irish in 1889 before dropping out the team until 1896. He returned to play in another defeat of the English but then had to wait three years for his next cap, and only defeat, against England in Birmingham. His international career appeared to be over but there was one last recall, more than 16 years after his first cap, when Scotland defeated England 2-1 at Bramall Lane in 1903. Second-half goals just three minutes apart from Finlay Speedie and Robert Walker secured the victory after Scotland had trailed at half-time.

MONDAY 4TH APRIL 1921

Billy Houliston, the only Queen of the South player to earn a full Scottish cap, was born in Dumfries in 1921. His contribution to Queens, both as a player and then later as chairman, was massive but he struggled to make an impact at international level despite a sensational debut in 1948 against Ireland. He scored twice in that game, including a last-gasp winner, as Scotland came back from two goals down to win 3-2 and this earned him further caps against England and France in 1949. Commentators and fans were critical of his performance against the English and though he took part in an unofficial tour, his international career was over.

SATURDAY 5TH APRIL 1879

Scotland had a bad day at the office in 1879 as they led England 4-1 thanks to goals from John McDougall, John Smith and a double from William MacKinnon, yet still contrived to lose 5-4 as England staged a dramatic comeback. The hosts had opened the scoring but four unanswered goals seemed to have the visitors heading for victory until the match changed after the break. It remains the only loss suffered by the team having led by three goals.

SATURDAY 5TH APRIL 1902

Tragedy struck Scottish football when 26 people lost their lives in the Ibrox disaster. The newly constructed West Terracing (at what is now the Broomloan Road end of the ground), which consisted of wooden strips supported by a steel frame, was weakened by heavy rain the night before the match against England and collapsed under the weight of spectators early in the second half. Some fans fell up to 12 metres through the gaping terrace to the ground below while others were left dangling from the shredded wooden steps and steel girders as they waited to be rescued. Along with the dead, more than 500 people were also treated for other injuries. The contractor who built the terrace was taken to court but though cleared of charges, the disaster did force changes to the construction of football grounds at the time as wooden terracing of this design was banned. It was replaced by terraces either built on top of earth piling or reinforced concrete. The match, the first Scotland–England encounter between two completely professional teams, eventually finished in a 1-1 draw but was declared void by the SFA and FA and replayed at Villa Park, Birmingham, around a month later. The proceeds from the second match went to a fund which supported families affected by the disaster.

SATURDAY 5TH APRIL 1952

Scotland have played a total of five games on April 5th, all against England, and have failed to win any of them. The final attempt was in 1952 but despite Lawrie Reilly's goal at Hampden Park the side still went down 2-1. They did manage one home draw, in 1890, but suffered other defeats in 1879, 1913 and 1930.

SATURDAY 6TH APRIL 1895

The Auld Enemy clash of 1895 threw up a couple of quirks as Scotland went down to a 3-0 defeat. David Russell of Hearts became the first player to be capped on his birthday while Neil Gibson of Rangers became the first Scottish player to score an own goal.

SATURDAY 6TH APRIL 1963

Scotland's 2-1 win at Wembley was especially impressive as it was achieved with ten men. Eric Caldow suffered a broken leg in the contest early on and with no substitutes available Scotland had to soldier on without him. Caldow, who had been captain for three years, never played for Scotland again after the injury.

SATURDAY 7TH APRIL 1900

Robert McColl scored three goals against England in the 4-1 win of 1900 and became the first of three players to score three hat-tricks for Scotland. The others are Hughie Gallacher and Denis Law. The side used the primrose and pink striped racing colours of Lord Rosebery in this match as they did on many occasions around this time. Lord Rosebery was a former British Prime Minister and Honorary President of the SFA.

SATURDAY 7TH APRIL 1906

The latest version of Hampden hosted an international match for the first time in 1906 when a then world record crowd of 102,741 turned up to watch Scotland defeat England 2-1. Hampden would increase its own record several times before the Second World War but construction of the gigantic Maracanã in Rio de Janeiro meant the crowd title was lost forever.

WEDNESDAY 7TH APRIL 1976

The phrase 'dream debut' can be applied to Willie Pettigrew who scored the only goal of a friendly match against Switzerland in 1976. The Motherwell striker donned dark blue for the first time and needed only two minutes on the pitch to find the net, claiming the quickest debut goal in the history of Scottish international football. Scotland won the game 1-0 and Pettigrew was capped four more times, scoring another goal.

THURSDAY 8TH APRIL 1971

Manager Bobby Brown announced his squad to face Portugal in a forthcoming European Championship qualifier and took drastic action after the previous match which had resulted in a 3-0 defeat against Belgium. Charlie Cooke, Colin Stein and Archie Gemmill were axed but the manager had further problems as Leeds United declared Billy Bremner, Peter Lorimer and Eddie Gray would be unavailable to Scotland even though England had taken four players from the Elland Road club.

SATURDAY 9TH APRIL 1949

Scotland's fourth highest goalscorer of all-time is Lawrie Reilly and he found the net for his country for the first time in a 3-1 win over England at Wembley on this day. Reilly's goal, Scotland's third after strikes from Jimmy Mason and Billy Steel, clinched not only the match but the Home Championship as well. This was his third cap but having taken a little time to get going in the scoring stakes, he certainly made up for it with a sensational record which eventually resulted in 22 goals from 38 games. Though Reilly is fourth in the goal chart, he has a better scoring ratio than both Law and Dalglish with only Hugh Gallacher having a better rate in the top five scorers. Unfortunately, injury ended his career prematurely and he missed out on a probable berth at the 1958 World Cup as a result.

THURSDAY 9TH APRIL 2009

Few countries can match Scotland for drinking scandals and the 'bevvygate' debacle of 2009 took another twist on this day. Having been dropped to the bench for a match against Iceland as punishment for drinking heavily after a loss in Holland, Allan McGregor and Barry Ferguson compounded their error by making V signs at the press while sitting at Hampden. After being banned 'for life', SFA Chief Executive Gordon Smith signalled at lunchtime that circumstances might change and they could be welcomed back into the fold. Only hours later he reiterated they would not be considered for selection but it turned out the first change of heart was correct. Craig Levein, George Burley's successor as manager, quickly made it clear both players would be considered, though Ferguson eventually declined to come back into the national set-up.

THURSDAY 10TH APRIL 1930

Tommy Younger who would go on to keep goal for Scotland and become president of the SFA, was born in Edinburgh. He resumed his football career by returning from military service to play for Hibs and he soon proved himself to be an exceptional goalkeeper, winning two league titles and securing his position for Scotland. A move to Liverpool followed but the Anfield side were not yet the great club they would become and more honours, though not Scotland caps, were elusive. After retiring Younger eventually joined the board of Hibs and soon made an impression off the field as he progressed through the ranks of the SFA to become vice-president and finally president, representing the Scottish game until his death in 1984.

MONDAY 10TH APRIL 1967

The Scottish team was named for the coming clash with England on Saturday. A debut would be handed to 36-year-old goalkeeper Ronnie Simpson which made him the oldest player to ever start his Scotland career. Ironically, he made his league debut for Queen's Park against Clyde aged only 14 as the now Scotland manager Bobby Brown could not get leave from the armed forces to claim his usual spot between the posts! The team line-up also contained a debutant at the other end of the park as young Jim McCalliog would partner Denis Law in attack.

SATURDAY 11TH APRIL 1964

Beating England was always cause for celebration in Glasgow but there was some additional *Schadenfreude* available in 1964. Alan Gilzean's goal secured a 1-0 victory to ensure England would only share the Home Championship with Scotland rather than win it outright. However, Northern Ireland beating Wales a few days later ensured it would be a three-way tie with the Welsh finishing last.

SATURDAY 12TH APRIL 1924

Scotland played under the iconic twin towers of Wembley for the first time and secured a 1-1 draw. Willie Cowan, playing his only full international, scored just before the break to give the Scots the lead but an equaliser by Billy Walker after the interval ensured a share of the spoils.

SATURDAY 13TH APRIL 1889

Scotland became comeback kings as they overturned a two-goal deficit to win for the first time. England led 2-0 at half-time but goals from Neil Munro, James Oswald and James McLaren gave the Scots a dramatic victory.

SATURDAY 13TH APRIL 1929

Cheeky Alec Cheyne scored the winning goal for Scotland against England in 1929 when he fired home directly from a last-minute corner. It was the first international goal scored in this manner, coming only a couple of years after the rules had been changed to make it legal.

SATURDAY 13TH APRIL 1946

Victory Internationals in the immediate aftermath of the Second World War were not deemed official games but that didn't stop a mammoth crowd of 139,642 turning up at Hampden to watch Scotland play England. Jimmy Delaney was the hero of the day as he scored the only goal in the final minute of the contest to hand the hosts a 1-0 win. As far as the SFA is concerned, Delaney did collect 15 official caps and scored six goals in total. However, the outside-right also holds the distinction of winning cup medals in Scotland, England and Northern Ireland before losing a final in the Republic of Ireland.

MONDAY 13TH APRIL 1964

Scotland goalkeeper Andy Goram was born in Bury. He immediately impressed at his local club and having been called into the Scotland squad he became the first Athletic player to go to the World Cup finals in 1986, though he did not play in Mexico. He had moved north of the border before another non-playing trip to the World Cup in 1990 but with Jim Leighton suffering a crisis in form it was Goram between the posts for Euro 92. Goram was also given the nod by Craig Brown at Euro 96 and rewarded his manager with a stunning performance in the 0-0 draw with Holland. However, he withdrew from the training camp in America before the 1998 World Cup meaning that the international career of one of Scotland's finest-ever goalkeepers ended in disappointing fashion.

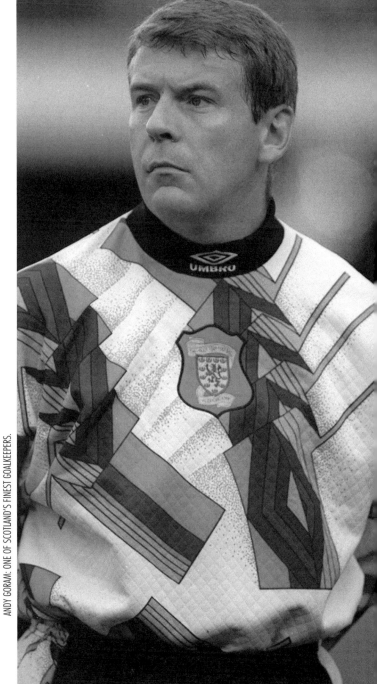

SATURDAY 14TH APRIL 1923

Andrew Wilson bagged one of the goals in a 2-2 draw with England to equal his own record of having scored in five successive matches. He had previously achieved the feat earlier in the 1920s but after failing to score against Wales in 1922, he immediately set off on a similar run with goals in the next five internationals.

SATURDAY 14TH APRIL 1945

The shortest international career in history surely belongs to Alex Bogan. He started a wartime international – so is not included in official records – against England in 1945 but crashed into English goalkeeper Frank Swift in the first attack. The unfortunate Alex immediately left the field with ligament damage and was never selected for Scotland again.

SATURDAY 14TH APRIL 1956

Scotland were denied the Home Championship when Johnny Haynes scored with just seconds remaining to secure a 1-1 draw at Hampden. Either side would have won the championship with victory in this match but the draw meant the tournament was shared between all four nations for the only time in history. Scotland handed a debut to South African defender John Hewie. He had Scottish parents, but his first steps in the country were to represent the national team! Hewie could be pleased with his impressive debut which included an assist to Graham Leggat for the opening goal.

THURSDAY 14TH APRIL 1983

One of Scotland's most recent heroes, James McFadden, was born in 1983. The young Faddy made a massive impact as he broke through the ranks at Motherwell and had already been capped by the national side when he secured a £1.25m move to Everton in 2003, before moving on to Birmingham City in 2008. McFadden has always produced his best for Scotland and a run of goals in the qualifying campaign for Euro 2008 – including the sensational winner in Paris against France – endeared him to the fans. Although not an out-and-out striker, McFadden has already notched 15 goals for his country and has the potential to move further up the all-time scorers' list from his current sixth position.

SATURDAY 15TH APRIL 1939

A massive crowd of nearly 150,000 crammed into Hampden to watch a mud fight between Scotland and England end in a 2-1 win for the visitors. The condition of the pitch was so bad the players changed shirts at half-time with the English, who only had one kit of their own, borrowing a spare set from Queen's Park!

SATURDAY 15TH APRIL 1950

Fifa offered places at the World Cup in Brazil to the top two sides in the 1950 Home Championship. However, the SFA, in a decision which now seems mind-boggling, stated Scotland would only travel if they won the championship. They were left to regret the decision as Scotland – needing only a home draw to claim the title – lost 1-0 to England at Hampden. Despite both captains on the day, George Young and Billy Wright, pleading with the SFA to change the decision, Scotland stayed at home that summer.

SATURDAY 15TH APRIL 1961

England 9-3 Scotland – let's just skip it.

SATURDAY 15TH APRIL 1967

If the 9-3 match represents one of the all-time lows in Scottish football, the lesson dished out to England at Wembley six years later is one of the high points. Scotland may have won only 3-2 but the close result belied just how completely dominant the visitors were in this game. Had Gordon Banks not been in form, the final scoreline would have been much higher in favour of the Scots. England were on a long unbeaten run at home but were left chasing shadows, particularly in the second half, when Scotland began mocking the world champions as Jim Baxter, Billy Bremner and Denis Law delighted the huge Scottish support with an outrageous series of backheels, flicks and keepie-uppies. The match was particularly sweet revenge for Denis Law, the only Scot to feature in the 9-3 game, and he opened the scoring before Bobby Lennox and Jim McCalliog added further goals. The full team was: Ronnie Simpson, Tommy Gemmell, Eddie McCreadie, John Greig, Ronnie McKinnon, Jim Baxter, Willie Wallace, Billy Bremner, Jim McCalliog, Denis Law, and Bobby Lennox.

WEDNESDAY 16TH APRIL 1975

Scotland managed a 1-1 draw against Sweden in a Gothenburg friendly which saw Colin Jackson make his debut. The defender played only eight times for Scotland but was a good-luck charm – he was never on a losing side. He helped draw further games against Wales and Romania while he tasted victory against Portugal, Denmark, Wales, Northern Ireland and England.

SATURDAY 17TH APRIL 1937

A then world record (and still standing European record) crowd of 149,547 arrived at Hampden Park to watch Scotland defeat England 3-1 in the British Home Championship. A Bob McPhail double and a goal by Francis O'Donnell secured the victory but it was only enough to earn Scotland second place in the championship table as Wales won all of their games that season. The Scottish Cup Final was also held at Hampden a week later and Celtic defeated Aberdeen 1-0 in front of 147,365, a current record for a European club match. Jimmy Delaney played in both games meaning he had performed in front of nearly 297,000 people in the space of eight days!

MONDAY 17TH APRIL 1967

After the glorious victory over England at the weekend, many Scots would have taken great delight at reading through the newspaper reports of the match. The *Glasgow Herald* started its report "England's mantle of invincibility was stripped from their shoulders" but the tone of the piece, while making Scotland's superiority clear, was not indulgent or hysterical compared to modern reports when Scotland achieve some form of success. The actions of the Scotland players were never forgotten though and when Jim Baxter died in 2001, respected football historian and journalist Bob Crampsey called his keepie-uppie at Wembley "a defining moment for almost every football fan in Scotland, irrespective of where their club allegiance lies".

SATURDAY 18TH APRIL 1953

'Last-minute Reilly' was the hero of the day as Scotland scored twice in the second half to claim a 2-2 draw with England at Wembley. Lawrie Reilly claimed both with the equaliser coming at the death to earn him his appropriate, if not overly snappy, nickname.

SATURDAY 19TH APRIL 1958

Scotland endured a heavy loss when they were hammered 4-0 at home to England in the British Home Championship. A home win would have given Scotland a share of the title with Northern Ireland but instead it was the English who had that honour after scoring twice in each half. This was Scotland's first game of the year and with the next two being a draw in Hungary and defeat in Poland, the side were not on a high going into the World Cup finals in the summer of 1958.

MONDAY 19TH APRIL 2010

Scottish football was coming to terms with the sudden resignation of SFA chief executive Gordon Smith on this day. It had been confirmed late in the previous evening that Smith was to leave his post, citing personal reasons, and the post-mortem was well and truly under way. Many commentators felt Smith possessed good ideas which he struggled to implement through the committee system of the SFA, an organisational hierarchy dating back decades. One lasting legacy was changing the rules governing which players could be considered for the Scotland team meaning those who moved to the country at a young age would be able to represent their adopted nation. Writing in *The Scotsman*, Alan Patullo surmised: "Scottish football will survive Gordon Smith's resignation as chief executive of the Scottish Football Association, but the game's governing body doesn't deserve to – at least not in its current guise."

WEDNESDAY 20TH APRIL 1994

As Scotland were not travelling to the 1994 World Cup, Craig Brown was already making plans for the Euro 96 qualifying campaign. Scotland's only victory during the first nine months of the year came in Vienna against Austria as John McGinlay and Billy McKinlay secured a 2-1 win.

WEDNESDAY 21ST APRIL 1971

Scotland's hopes of progressing from the qualifying group of the 1972 European Championships were dealt a blow when they lost 2-0 to Portugal in Lisbon. Pat Stanton's own goal, and then a late strike from Eusebio, proved decisive and a further loss in the next match effectively ended the campaign.

THURSDAY 22ND APRIL 2010

Scottish Television ran a series of programmes to decide Scotland's greatest-ever team. The caveat that players were only considered from 1967 onwards gave the team a decidedly modern slant but the public still voted for a formidable eleven. Andy Goram, Sandy Jardine, Willie Miller, Alex McLeish, Danny McGrain, Jimmy Johnstone, Billy Bremner, Graeme Souness, Davie Cooper, Denis Law and Kenny Dalglish were the men nominated with Jock Stein elected as manager.

WEDNESDAY 23RD APRIL 1986

Though Don Hutchison scored the winning goal for Scotland against England at Wembley in 1999, you have to look back a lot further to find the last Scottish-born player to score against the Auld Enemy. That honour falls to Graeme Souness who notched the Scottish consolation in the Rous Cup 2-1 defeat at Wembley in 1986. Despite suggestions of bringing back the Scotland–England fixture, if only for a one-off, it seems as if this record could stand for some time.

TUESDAY 24TH APRIL 1928

One of the best known figures in Scottish football, Tommy Docherty, was born on this day. While younger fans may only recognise 'The Doc' for his quick-witted one-liners, it should not be forgotten that he enjoyed a significant playing career, earning 25 caps, before becoming an accomplished manager. He took over the national team in 1971, earning two victories at the end of the 1972 European Championship qualifying campaign, and led the side to significant wins home and away against Denmark in World Cup 74 qualification before resigning his post to take charge at Manchester United late in 1972.

WEDNESDAY 25TH APRIL 2001

Scott Booth had scored five goals for Scotland but had to wait nearly six years to notch number six. After struggling for form he played his way back into international contention after moving to Holland and was recalled for a friendly in Poland. He slammed home a penalty to secure a 1-1 draw in Bydgoszcz but the renaissance was short. He played only another three matches, failing to score again, to end his career with six goals in 23 games.

WEDNESDAY 26TH APRIL 1972

Scotland met Peru for the first time in 1972 and comfortably defeated them 2-0 in a Hampden friendly. The goals were provided by John O'Hare and Denis Law but the visitors would more than extract revenge the next time the sides met, six years later in a World Cup encounter in Cordoba.

WEDNESDAY 26TH APRIL 1989

Scotland took a huge step towards qualifying for Italia 90 when they defeated Cyprus 2-1 at Hampden. The Cypriots had posed Scotland huge problems in the first meeting between the sides in Limassol but things were a little more straightforward this time. A breathtaking overhead kick by Mo Johnston opened the scoring and though the guests did manage to equalise, Ally McCoist bagged the winner. A strong run of form at the start of the campaign meant that Scotland now needed only one point from their last three games – away to Yugoslavia and France, home to Norway – to guarantee a place at the finals.

WEDNESDAY 27TH APRIL 1949

Scotland played France for four consecutive years between 1948 and 1951 and despite losing the first encounter in Paris, the next three matches would be won. The first of this run of victories came courtesy of two Billy Steel goals in front of over 120,000 at Hampden Park.

WEDNESDAY 27TH APRIL 1977

Joe Craig had not even kicked a ball for Scotland when his teammates were rushing to congratulate him for a goal on his debut. The Celtic striker was brought on as a substitute with Scotland leading Sweden 2-1, and before he had a chance to make an impact with his feet, he had headed a decisive third goal to ensure victory. Asa Hartford and Kenny Dalglish were also on the score-sheet but the lasting memory of the night was Craig's dramatic introduction. Unfortunately for him this would turn out to be his only international appearance and a year later he would leave Glasgow to sign for Blackburn Rovers. After helping them to promotion he returned to Hamilton but suffered through injuries and was forced to retire in 1983.

WEDNESDAY 28TH APRIL 1948

Davie Duncan of East Fife became the first lower league Scottish player to be selected for the national side when he played in a friendly against Belgium in 1948. He made an impressive start with a goal in the 2-0 victory but defeats in his next appearances against Switzerland and France drew the curtain on his international career.

WEDNESDAY 28TH APRIL 1993

In the long list of Scottish football disasters, the 5-0 defeat in Lisbon to Portugal features highly. It was the *coup de grace* to a dismal qualifying campaign which saw the team fail to reach the World Cup finals for the first time in 24 years.

WEDNESDAY 28TH APRIL 1999

Scotland victories against Germany are rare and the nation was boosted by this 1-0 friendly success in Bremen. Don Hutchison scored the only goal but this was not an omen of immediate success as the next match resulted in a disappointing draw in the Faroe Islands.

TUESDAY 29TH APRIL 1986

Scotland's 0-0 friendly draw with Holland will be remembered fondly by at least one legend – Ally McCoist. He made his debut and went on to win a further 60 caps, scoring 19 goals in the process. Notable strikes include the opener against Norway in 1989 to take the team to the World Cup in Italy and he also scored a crucial goal against Greece en route to Euro 96, notching another in the finals.

WEDNESDAY 30TH APRIL 1997

Scotland travelled to Sweden for an important World Cup qualifier at the end of April and turned in a poor performance to lose 2-1. Despite a late rally from the Scots, Sweden deserved the points but Scotland had the last laugh as they qualified for the finals in France. A number of fans showed their support for the SNP in the general election which was held the next day – they did a little better than Scotland on this occasion, gaining an extra two seats in Parliament.

WEDNESDAY 1ST MAY 1991

Scotland took on one of the new minnows of international football

SCOTLAND
On This Day

MAY

for the first time when they faced San Marino in Serravalle. While Scotland occasionally struggle in games they are expected to win comfortably they have always managed to come out on top against the side from the microstate. Sometimes there have been moments of concern on the way but in this instance goals from Gordon Strachan and Gordon Durie ensured there would be no slip-up on the path to the Swedish finals of Euro 92.

SUNDAY 2ND MAY 1937

Tommy Ewing was born on this day in Swinhill. He is not the most famous of Scottish players and the left-winger picked up only two caps. However, things could have been very different for him if national service had not prevented him being considered for the 1958 World Cup finals in Sweden.

WEDNESDAY 2ND MAY 1962

Scotland lost 3-2 at home to Uruguay in a match which was billed as a friendly but turned out to be anything but. Jim Baxter and Ralph Brand scored the goals for Scotland but the fans were also treated to a full-on brawl which saw the referee punched, apparently by an unidentified Scotland player. The trouble started when a Uruguayan, who was off the pitch with an injury, was moved back onto the field to hold up play. Pat Crerand and Baxter attempted to roll him off again but the Uruguayans reacted angrily and the police eventually came onto the pitch to separate the squabbling players. In the middle of the stooshie someone caught referee Arthur Holland and he was pictured, in the *Evening Times*, bent double from the mystery blow!

SATURDAY 3RD MAY 1969

Scotland's Home Championship of 1969 got off to a flying start with a 5-3 win in Wales. Billy McNeill and Colin Stein gave the guests a two-goal advantage but that had vanished before half-time. Alan Gilzean restored the lead for just two minutes but late goals from Billy Bremner and Tommy McLean ensured the points belonged to Scotland.

FRIDAY 4TH MAY 1984

Former Scotland player and manager Willie Ormond died on this day, aged 57. As an outside-left in Hibs' Famous Five, he came into the Scottish side in 1954 but after playing in both games in the World Cup finals he had to wait several years to receive his sixth and final cap. As a manager he impressed with St Johnstone before taking the Scotland job in 1973 following the departure of Tommy Docherty. He guided the team to the finals in West Germany where the side exited after the first round but were the only unbeaten team in the tournament, with one win and two draws to their credit.

WEDNESDAY 5TH MAY 1954

Before the disastrous World Cup of 1954 there were warning signs that Scotland might struggle. The first of three warm-up games was played at Hampden but in front of only 25,000 fans (over 130,000 had watched the England game a month earlier). The side laboured to a 1-0 win against Norway thanks to a George Hamilton goal. A draw in the return match in Oslo, and a narrow win in Helsinki a week later, completed a rather flat build-up to the tournament.

WEDNESDAY 6TH MAY 1959

West Germany visited Scotland in 1959 for the first time since the division of their country after World War II. A huge crowd witnessed a sensational first half an hour which featured five goals including one from the legendary Uwe Seeler. The Hamburg hero could not stop the Scots triumphing on the night as goals from John White, Andy Weir and Graham Leggat secured a 3-2 victory.

SUNDAY 7TH MAY 1961

Scotland started their campaign to reach the 1962 World Cup with two games in the space of a week against the Republic of Ireland. The first was won 4-1 at Hampden and the second, on this day, brought an equally comfortable success in Dublin. A goal from Ralph Brand, after Alex Young scored twice, helped set up two crunch clashes with Czechoslovakia which looked set to decide the winner of the group.

SUNDAY 8TH MAY 1932

Scotland met France for the second time in a Paris encounter in 1932 and maintained a 100 per cent record thanks to a 3-1 win. Neil Dewar of Third Lanark was the hero as his hat-trick ensured victory.

WEDNESDAY 8TH MAY 1963

A friendly match between Scotland and Austria descended into farce and the referee had to abandon this encounter during the second half because of the visitors' behaviour. After a Davie Wilson double, Nemec was booked and then sent off for spitting at the referee – but that was only the start. Denis Law scored a brace of his own before becoming the victim of a shocking challenge from Hof. He was also shown red but refused to leave the field until the police became involved. Law was again targeted, this time by Linhart, and his retaliation persuaded the referee that abandoning the game – with Scotland leading 4-1 – was the best way of ensuring no-one was seriously hurt. This common-sense approach infuriated many in the 90,000 crowd who angrily demanded their money back.

SUNDAY 9TH MAY 1937

Scotland had taken on Austria for potentially the last time in a 1937 friendly when Frank O'Donnell's goal secured a 1-1 draw in Vienna. Almost a year to the day in 1938, Austria was annexed by Nazi Germany.

WEDNESDAY 10TH MAY 1967

Scotland fans know that the inevitable follow-on from a glorious high is disappointment. After defeating world champions England in their last game, Scotland's poor performance saw them lose 2-0 to the USSR in the next match. European Cup winners Celtic provided seven players in the line-up for the first time since the war.

THURSDAY 11TH MAY 2006

Walter Smith's magic touch continued as the side hammered Bulgaria 5-1 in the opening game of the 2006 Kirin Cup. Doubles from Kris Boyd and Chris Burke, along with another goal from James McFadden, put Scotland in a dominant position before the final match against hosts Japan.

CHRIS BURKE SCORED A DOUBLE FOR SCOTLAND AGAINST BULGARIA IN 2006.

WEDNESDAY 12TH MAY 1982

Scotland striker Billy Steel died aged 59 in Los Angeles on this day. Steel was an impressive inside-forward who earned the first of his 30 Scottish caps against England in 1947 and did sufficiently well to earn a place in the British side which took on the Rest of Europe shortly afterwards. A British record transfer took him from Morton to Derby County before a Scottish record fee brought him back north of the border to Dundee. He helped them win two League Cups but tasted Scottish Cup final defeat against Motherwell in 1952. A banner in the crowd that day boasted Motherwell had been looking after Steel for years! From Dundee, Steel moved to America to play for two teams before continuing life after football in his adopted country.

THURSDAY 13TH MAY 1965

The SFA were desperate to secure qualification to the 1966 World Cup and after an unimpressive run of form manager Ian McColl was replaced by Jock Stein. Stein, who took the role on a part-time basis, recorded a famous victory over Italy at Hampden Park but dropped points against Poland meant qualification hinged on the final game in Naples. A 3-0 reverse, under circumstances which left him well short of his first-choice team, eliminated Scotland from the tournament and left Stein bitterly rueing the constraints placed upon the national manager.

SATURDAY 13TH MAY 2006

David Weir became the first Scotland captain in over 20 years to lift a trophy thanks to a 0-0 draw against Japan. A stout defensive performance had denied the Kirin Cup hosts the win they needed to claim the trophy. Scotland triumphed on goal difference thanks to their earlier 5-1 thrashing of Bulgaria.

MONDAY 14TH MAY 1934

Eric Caldow, one of Scotland's most inspirational captains, was born in Cumnock on this day. He had reached the 40-cap mark before his 30th birthday and was closing in on the appearance record held by George Young. However, a bad tackle at Wembley shattered that dream as it shattered his leg with a triple break.

MONDAY 15TH MAY 1967

The Scotland party, embarking on a world tour, departed from London. There was a blow for the group as Frank McClintock pulled out with injury but better news from north London was that Ian Ure had been given permission to take part in the whole tour. Another boost was that Sheffield Wednesday no longer required Jim McCalliog to leave the group in Los Angeles to meet up with their own tour in Mexico.

WEDNESDAY 15TH MAY 1974

A few days before the clash with England at Hampden the Scotland team were permitted by manager Willie Ormond to have a few drinks to aid team-bonding in Largs. On the way home Jimmy Johnstone jumped into a boat in the harbour and was larking around when – allegedly given a nudge by a colleague – he drifted off towards the sea. With no oars to direct him back to shore, Johnstone was potentially in danger. The coastguard was called to perform a rescue but sympathy for the wee man was thin on the ground; an outraged press demanded he be dropped. Instead, Ormond kept faith with the winger and he was inspired as Scotland coasted to a 2-0 victory.

SATURDAY 16TH MAY 1931

For the first time Scotland lost to a non-home nation and did so in style, hammered 5-0 by Austria in Vienna. The Wunderteam proved way too strong for the beleaguered Scots with three goals before half-time effectively ending the contest. Matthias Sindelar, arguably the greatest Austrian footballer of all time, scored the fourth.

WEDNESDAY 16TH MAY 1951

The pink and primrose racing colours of Lord Rosebery were used by Scotland for the last time in a 1-0 win against France. Archibald Primrose was born in 1847 and was a successful politician in the Liberal party, enjoying a short spell as Prime Minister in the 1890s. He would later become Honorary President of the SFA but his involvement with football was long established having donated a charity cup to be played for among East of Scotland teams in 1882.

SATURDAY 17TH MAY 1969

Scotland posted their record win in the post-war era with an 8-0 thrashing of Cyprus at Hampden. The headlines were stolen by Colin Stein who bagged four goals, taking the number of Scottish hat-tricks to 36. Stein became the 29th – and to date the last – player to score a treble.

MONDAY 18TH MAY 1857

Andrew Watson, believed to be the world's first black footballer, was born on this day in British Guiana. The son of a Scottish sugar planter, he moved to Scotland where he attended Glasgow University and played three times for the national team in 1881, the first of which was in a victory away to England. After gaining his degree he later moved to Australia where he spent the rest of his life. It is not known exactly when he died.

THURSDAY 18TH MAY 1972

With Hampden Park urgently in need of repair, an appeal to save the ground came from an unlikely source – Celtic. The club proposed that a combination of the SFA, the SFL and the Old Firm stumped up £120,000 between them to get things going. Celtic had thoughtfully invited Rangers into the scheme since they believed the only other club of their stature in Scotland would not wish to be embarrassed by being left out!

WEDNESDAY 18TH MAY 1977

Scottish football changed forever with the appointment of Ally MacLeod as manager in 1977. The larger-than-life character had done well in charge of Ayr United and had led Aberdeen to the League Cup before being handed the national job. He started brightly. The British Home Championship was won in sensational fashion at Wembley before Scotland knocked out European champions Czechoslovakia to reach the 1978 World Cup finals. MacLeod whipped the nation into a frenzy and the belief that Scotland would finish in the top three simply made the first-round exit all the more crushing. He departed after only one more match but the interest that he had created in the team was unprecedented and he is very fondly remembered by the vast majority of Scottish fans.

THE REDEVELOPMENT OF HAMPDEN PARK WAS A CONTENTIOUS ISSUE FOR DECADES BEFORE WORK IN THE 1990S TURNED IT INTO A MODERN STADIUM.

SUNDAY 19TH MAY 1957

Scotland maintained a 100 per cent record in the race to qualify for the World Cup in Sweden in 1958 with a 2-1 win in Switzerland. Having defeated Spain at Hampden, the team travelled to Basel and returned home with the points thanks to goals from Jackie Mudie and Bobby Collins. Captain George Young, who had become the first player to win 50 caps, extended the appearance record to 53 in this match but he was controversially – and allegedly without explanation – dropped from the final qualifying games and not recalled.

WEDNESDAY 19TH MAY 1971

Only hours after Scotland suffered a home defeat to Northern Ireland, Hampden Park was ripped up. The SFA had not become disgracefully bad losers and despite the disappointment of the previous result the measure was only temporary – fresh turf would be laid after new drainage had been installed.

SATURDAY 20TH MAY 1972

Denis Law scored his last international goal in a 2-0 victory against Northern Ireland. This was his 30th goal in 44 games but although he would earn another 11 caps and play in the successful qualifying campaign for the 1974 World Cup, he would not find the net again. Law did make an appearance at the World Cup finals in West Germany, playing against Zaire, but he was coming to the end of his career and this turned out to be his final game before retiring. Law never played for a Scottish club and although he was inducted into the English Football Hall of Fame in 2002 he is one of the proudest players ever to have pulled on the dark blue shirt of his country. In 2010 he was made patron of the charity Football Aid.

SATURDAY 21ST MAY 1977

Scottish international Martin Buchan made history in 1977 when he became the first man to captain cup-winning teams either side of the border. Aged only 21 he had become the youngest Scottish Cup-winning captain when Aberdeen defeated Celtic 3-1 in 1970 and he repeated the trick when Manchester United claimed a 2-1 success over Liverpool at Wembley on this day.

MONDAY 22ND MAY 2000

Scotland manager Craig Brown was a man in demand. He had been offered a job as manager of Hong Kong but explained to the *Scotsman* newspaper he was going nowhere – though added a couple of bad results could take the decision out of his hands!

SATURDAY 23RD MAY 1981

In the British Home Championship of 1981 only Scotland completed their full schedule of fixtures. The last of those was a 1-0 win against England thanks to John Robertson's penalty but the tournament was abandoned as England and Wales refused to travel to Belfast because of sectarian troubles.

SATURDAY 23RD MAY 1998

Scotland continued to prepare for the World Cup with a 2-2 draw against Colombia. Goals from John Collins and Craig Burley were cancelled out by an early penalty and late equaliser as Scotland impressed the South Americans with a patient passing style.

THURSDAY 23RD MAY 2002

Scotland ended their Eastern tour with a 4-0 thrashing of a Hong Kong XI. The level of opposition was well below that of South Korea and South Africa, who had beaten Scotland in previous games and the fixture is not officially recognised by Fifa. The SFA gave it full international status so scorers Kevin Kyle, Steven Thompson, Christian Dailly and Scot Gemmill had their goals added to their career totals.

MONDAY 24TH MAY 2010

The SFA ended a long-running sponsorship deal with Tennent's Lager as it decided to look for new business opportunities. The Scottish brewery had been involved with football for decades dating back to the Tennent's Sixes in the 1980s and had been a backer of the national team. However, Tennent's sponsorship of the Old Firm caused a re-evaluation of their involvement with the SFA and it was decided an amicable parting of ways was for the best. On the same day the SFA also announced the Scotland Supporters' Club had reached the 35,000 mark making it one of the biggest of its kind in Europe.

SATURDAY 25TH MAY 1974

Having reached the finals of the World Cup for the first time in 16 years, Scotland were determined to make the most of their trip to West Germany in 1974. The squad recorded a novelty song to celebrate the trip and their effort, Easy Easy, is recorded by chartstats.com as appearing in the album chart for the first time on this day. It entered at position 13 – not bad for something containing the line 'Yabadabadoo, we support the boys in the blue'!

THURSDAY 25TH MAY 1978

The country witnessed extraordinary scenes on this day as Scotland departed from Hampden Park to win the World Cup in Argentina. Or so it was thought. A crowd of 30,000 not only turned up at the ground, but paid for the privilege of entry, as pipe bands, dancing girls and Andy Cameron provided the warm up to the main event – which was the slightly low-key introduction of the players and then a couple of laps round the park in an open-top bus. The event was shown live on television before the players made their way to Prestwick Airport along streets and, even more remarkably, the usually empty moors of Ayrshire, which were lined with people. If they only knew what would happen in Argentina!

SATURDAY 25TH MAY 1985

Scotland won the Rous Cup for the only time when they defeated England 1-0 at a rain-soaked Hampden Park. Richard Gough's looping header was the decisive moment in the game and allowed captain Graeme Souness to collect what would turn out to be Scotland's last trophy for 21 years.

SUNDAY 26TH MAY 1929

After several decades of playing only England, Wales and Ireland, Scotland broadened horizons by embarking on a tour. The first opponents from outside of the British Isles were Norway who were beaten 7-3 in Bergen. Alec Cheyne claimed a hat-trick in the victory on this day, with other goals coming from Robert Rankin, Thomas Craig and James Nisbet, who scored two, as the Scots looked on towards Germany and Holland.

SATURDAY 27TH MAY 1950

When Allan Brown scored the only goal of the game to give Scotland a 1-0 win in Paris, few people would have imagined it would be the last Scottish victory away to France for 57 years. That long record was broken with James McFadden's wonder goal in 2007 though it is not quite as bad as it seems – just four matches were lost in this time.

SUNDAY 27TH MAY 1951

Billy Steel holds an admirable tally of 12 Scotland goals in 30 games but also one record of which he will not be so proud. During a 4-0 defeat to Austria in Vienna, Swiss referee Jean Lutz dismissed Steel from the field for reacting angrily to conceding a free kick and tripping his opponent after the whistle sounded. Scotland, frustrated with their performance, were lucky not to have more players sent off.

FRIDAY 28TH MAY 1982

The Scotland under-18 side reached the semi-final of the European Championship held in Finland thanks to wins over Turkey and Albania and a draw in the final group game against Holland – despite a goal from Marco Van Basten. The Scots met Poland and triumphed 2-0 to move into Sunday's final against Czechoslovakia.

WEDNESDAY 28TH MAY 1997

Paul Lambert became the first Scot to win the European Cup with an overseas club when Borussia Dortmund defeated Juventus 3-1 in Munich in 1997. Lambert had impressed the Germans when playing against them for Motherwell in the Uefa Cup but few expected him to become a regular in their star-studded side.

FRIDAY 28TH MAY 2010

The European Championship began as a modest tournament in 1958 but the finals of the competition have gradually increased from four teams to eight, then 16 and, from 2016, 24. The new-look finals were awarded to France on this day, as their bid defeated Turkey by just one vote in the final ballot. Surely Scotland can qualify for finals which feature nearly half the teams on the continent!

SUNDAY 29TH MAY 1955

Scotland played only one game in Europe outside of Glasgow which had an official attendance in six figures. A crowd of 102,000 was inside the Népstadion – now renamed in honour of the great Ferenc Puskás – in Budapest to watch Hungary face Scotland. However, the visitors did not make a winning impression on the locals, losing 3-1. Gordon Smith gave Scotland the lead but Hungary fought back with goals from Nandor Hidegkuti, Sandor Kocsis and Mate Fenyvesi. Puskás also played in the match.

SUNDAY 29TH MAY 1960

Austria defeated Scotland 4-1 in a Vienna friendly when Alex Young of Hearts made history as the first-ever Scottish substitute. He entered the fray after only 12 minutes, replacing the injured Denis Law.

SATURDAY 29TH MAY 1982

Scotland lost 1-0 to England in 1982 but the SFA used the match programme to explain why Scotland the Brave would be used as the anthem in the coming World Cup. They were 'convinced it would be in Scotland's interest for the Scottish team to be identified in Spain by a Scottish tune rather than a British tune...'

SUNDAY 30TH MAY 1982

Scotland sealed their only official title to date when they defeated Czechoslovakia 3-1 in the final of the under-18 European Championships. Goals from John Philliben, Pat Nevin and Gary Mackay – all of whom had long football careers – proved decisive, as the Czechs could only muster a solitary strike from Kula in return. There were several notable names in the side including captain Paul McStay, who would win 76 senior caps, while coaches Andy Roxburgh and Walter Smith would both manage the full international team.

FRIDAY 31ST MAY 2002

The deadline had arrived for bids to host Euro 2008. After initially attempting a solo bid, the SFA eventually pitched in with Ireland but faced stern competition from several other countries. Unfortunately, Scotland and Ireland were eliminated early in the voting and the tournament was given to Austria and Switzerland.

SCOTLAND
On This Day

JUNE

SUNDAY 1st JUNE 1997

Scotland were gearing up for a crucial World Cup qualifier in Belarus and the gap between that game and the domestic season ending was filled by a friendly against Malta in Valletta. A goal from Christian Dailly, and a Darren Jackson double, ensured a 3-2 victory.

SATURDAY 2nd JUNE 1979

Hampden was the setting as football history was written in 1979. Diego Maradona scored his first international goal as world champions Argentina defeated Scotland 3-1 in a summer friendly. Hampden would remain significant for him as his first game as the Argentinian manager would take place there nearly 30 years later.

WEDNESDAY 2nd JUNE 1993

There was finally some light relief in the World Cup qualifying campaign of 1994 when Estonia made their first visit to Scotland for a game in Aberdeen. A brace from Pat Nevin, and another from Brian McClair, secured a 3-1 victory but Scotland's struggles against better teams in the group – Italy, Portugal and Switzerland – would prove fatal.

SUNDAY 3rd JUNE 1956

Future Scotland player and manager George Burley was born on this day in Cumnock. He is mainly associated with Ipswich Town, for whom he played in their glory days of the 1970s and 1980s. He also had a successful spell as manager of the Portman Road club. He gained 11 full Scottish caps and was appointed manager of the national team in 2008. He had an unconvincing start as three friendly matches failed to bring a win before the 2010 World Cup campaign and poor performances in that tournament eventually cost him his job.

SATURDAY 3rd JUNE 1978

The supposed march to the latter stages of the 1978 World Cup started when Scotland faced Peru in Cordoba. Joe Jordan opened the scoring early on but Peru fought back and levelled before half-time. Don Masson's missed penalty after the break was a turning point and two stunning goals from distance by Teofilis Cubillas handed Peru a 3-1 victory.

SATURDAY 4TH JUNE 1977

One of Scotland's most famous victories occurred when they defeated England 2-1 at Wembley in 1977 thanks to goals from Gordon McQueen and Kenny Dalglish. The former had opened the scoring with a powerful header from a free kick while the latter scored what turned out to be the winner by forcing the ball over the line following a frantic scramble. England pulled one back with a late penalty but had no time for an equaliser to deny the guests what had been a deserved victory over the 90 minutes. Ally MacLeod was not yet leading his army to Argentina but an early indication of the hysteria to come was seen when the ecstatic Scottish supporters poured onto the pitch to celebrate victory. The players were congratulated before the fans began taking souvenirs of the day as chunks of the Wembley pitch were dug up and duly re-laid in gardens all over Scotland. A particularly enthusiastic group started climbing over the goal posts at one end of the park and, predictably, the weight of so many fans eventually caused the cross bar to snap. Whether these events are viewed as disgraceful hooliganism or joyous celebrations generally depends on which side of Hadrian's Wall you were born but regardless the images of the day remain iconic on both sides of the border.

WEDNESDAY 4TH JUNE 1986

Scotland began their 1986 World Cup campaign in the so-called group of death alongside Denmark, West Germany and Uruguay. The first game was against Denmark and in a close contest it was the Danes who grabbed the only goal of the game as Elkjær Larsen found the net midway through the second half to claim victory.

SATURDAY 5TH JUNE 1998

After missing the 1994 World Cup finals in America, Scotland were eager to make a big impression on the tournament which was held in France four years later. The squad arrived in the small town of Saint-Remy-de-Provence on this day and they immediately formed a mutual appreciation society with the locals as the French population offered the visitors a warm welcome and were rewarded by having a relaxed team in their midst, who happily posed for pictures and signed autographs.

WEDNESDAY 6th JUNE 2007

Scotland looked to maintain the momentum of their Euro 2008 qualifying campaign when they headed to the Faroe Islands. Shaun Maloney opened the scoring with a lovely free kick, and Garry O'Connor doubled the lead, but there were nervous moments after the break as the hosts hit the woodwork before Scotland claimed the points.

WEDNESDAY 7th JUNE 1978

If Scotland fans doubted things could get worse after the loss to Peru at the 1978 World Cup finals, they were soon proved wrong. Scotland found the net just once against Iran, due to a comical own goal, and that was only enough to secure a point as Iran equalised later. Furious fans demanded their money back as the players left the pitch with Scotland's grand ambitions seemingly in tatters.

SUNDAY 8th JUNE 1958

Scotland enjoyed their first-ever goal in the World Cup finals when Jimmy Murray scored against Yugoslavia in Vasterås in 1958. It was his only international goal but it was not enough to provide a basis for victory as the Yugoslavs managed to ensure a share of the spoils in what was the opening game for both teams.

SUNDAY 8th JUNE 1986

After losing to Denmark in their opening game, Scotland faced another tough challenge in Mexico against West Germany. Gordon Strachan opened the scoring with the aid of a deflection but once more the Scots lost out in a tight contest as Rudi Völler and Klaus Allofs ensured a comeback victory for the Germans. Scotland's hopes of progressing would now hinge on the final game with Uruguay.

SUNDAY 8th JUNE 1997

Scotland's World Cup hopes were still in the balance when they headed to Minsk to take on Belarus for the first time in the summer of 1997. Almost a year after missing a penalty against England in Euro 96, Gary McAllister took responsibility for another crucial spot kick and this time found the top corner as Scotland achieved a crucial 1-0 win.

SHAUN MALONEY SCORED A FINE FREE KICK FOR SCOTLAND IN THE FAROE ISLANDS.

WEDNESDAY 9TH JUNE 1999

Scotland lost having led by two goals for the first time in 79 years as they went down 3-2 against the Czech Republic. Goals from Paul Ritchie and Allan Johnston had put Scotland en route to an unlikely away win but they were denied by a late comeback.

MONDAY 10TH JUNE 1996

Scotland held Holland to a goalless draw in Birmingham as they started the finals of Euro 96. Scotland had chances but it took a superb display of goalkeeping from Andy Goram to secure a point. John Collins also helped out by clearing the ball from the line with his arm without being punished.

WEDNESDAY 10TH JUNE 1998

The eyes of the world were on Scotland when they faced Brazil in the opening game of the 1998 World Cup. Despite trailing, Scotland played well and John Collins' penalty levelled the scores at half-time. Scotland deserved a draw but an unfortunate ricochet off Tom Boyd gave Brazil a late winner.

SUNDAY 11TH JUNE 1978

After the previous disasters against Peru and Iran, Scotland had to defeat Holland by three clear goals to reach the second round of the 1978 World Cup. The Dutch went in front but Kenny Dalglish and Archie Gemmill, with a penalty, turned the game around. Gemmill then wrote himself into folklore with a wonderful goal, jinking in from the right and beating several men before finishing superbly, leaving Scotland just one short of qualifying. It was not to be as Holland promptly scored again but dignity was restored at the end of a shocking campaign which also included Willie Johnston being sent home for failing a drug test.

MONDAY 11TH JUNE 1990

Scotland fans should know no opposition can be taken for granted but most expected Costa Rica to be defeated in the 1990 World Cup finals. More agony was ahead though as Scotland missed several chances and a goal against the run of play gave Costa Rica a 1-0 victory.

MONDAY 12TH JUNE 1989

In 1989 the under-17 World Cup was hosted in Scotland and took the nation by storm. Scotland won 3-0 against Cuba on this day at a packed Fir Park and draws against Ghana and Bahrain in the other group games allowed them to progress to the quarter-finals.

FRIDAY 12TH JUNE 1992

Scotland's first match at the finals of a European Championship took place in Gothenburg in 1992. Holland ran out narrow 1-0 winners but the day turned out to be a long one for Ally McCoist and Stewart McKimmie. They had to stay behind to participate in drug tests after the match and missed the plane carrying the team on to Norrköping as a result.

FRIDAY 13TH JUNE 1986

Uruguay blocked Scotland's path to the second round at the 1986 World Cup finals as the South Americans only needed a draw in this final group game to progress, while the Scots had to win. Despite Jose Batista being sent off after a record 55 seconds for assaulting Gordon Strachan, Uruguay successfully broke up play and frustrated their opponents. Steve Nicol missed a glorious chance in the second half but once more Scotland exited the tournament with a whimper rather than a bang.

SATURDAY 13TH JUNE 1998

Lessons had been learned in the recording studio, as well as on the park, from the World Cup of 1978 as Del Amitri's official song Don't Come Home Too Soon entered the charts. In stark contrast to the bubbling optimism of Ally's Tartan Army this was a sadly all too realistic appraisal of the team's chances at the finals.

FRIDAY 14TH JUNE 1974

Scotland started their first World Cup finals in 16 years with a match against Zaire in Dortmund. Goals from Peter Lorimer, who scored a superb volley, and Joe Jordan, with a header, secured the points but naively the Scots eased up to save energy rather than trying to score more. It would be a costly error.

SUNDAY 15TH JUNE 1958

After losing 3-2 to Paraguay in the middle group game of the 1958 World Cup, Scotland were on the verge of being knocked out when they faced France in Örebro to conclude the group. That picture did not change in the first half as France scored twice and despite Sammy Baird scoring in the second half Scotland finished bottom of the group once more.

TUESDAY 15TH JUNE 1982

The World Cup in 1982 started with a bang for Scotland as they hammered New Zealand in Malaga. However, after going out of the last two World Cups on goal difference it seemed especially careless to lose concentration and concede two goals when running the game at 3-0 up. Kenny Dalglish opened the scoring before John Wark scored a double before the break. After New Zealand's goals John Robertson and Steve Archibald increased the advantage once more but there would be much stiffer resistance from Brazil and the Soviet Union in the next two games.

MONDAY 15TH JUNE 1992

Scotland exited Euro 92 with their second successive loss as they went down 2-0 to Germany. There was no disgrace in losing to the world champions – and eventual tournament finalists – as they made the game safe only with a fluke goal when a cross was deflected over Andy Goram and unfortunately dropped just inside the back post.

SATURDAY 15TH JUNE 1996

After starting Euro 96 with a draw against Holland, Scotland were optimistic when they headed south to London to face England in the second game. The hosts had disappointed in their own opener against Switzerland so this clash was crucial to the outcome of the group. An unremarkable first half was followed by Alan Shearer opening the scoring early in the second period, but Scotland slowly took control. Gordon Durie had a header superbly saved and when Scotland won a penalty, a deserved equaliser looked likely. Gary McAllister's kick was blocked by goalkeeper Seaman and when Paul Gascoigne scored a magnificent goal on the counter-attack seconds later, Scotland were left to contemplate what might have been.

GARY MCALLISTER SHOWED GREAT COURAGE TO TAKE A CRUCIAL PENALTY AGAINST ENGLAND BUT COULD NOT FIND THE NET.

WEDNESDAY 16TH JUNE 1954

Scotland played their first-ever match in the World Cup finals against Austria in 1954. Though not as strong as the 1930s Wunderteam, they were still formidable opponents who had beaten Scotland twice three years previously without conceding a goal. On this occasion there was only one goal scored in Zurich but it came from an Austrian as they triumphed 1-0. Manager Andy Beattie, frustrated at restrictions placed on him by the SFA, would resign before the second group game against Uruguay.

SATURDAY 16TH JUNE 1990

After defeat in the first game in Group C of the 1990 World Cup, Scotland desperately needed to beat Sweden to get back on track, especially as the final match was against Brazil. Stuart McCall slid home an early opener from a corner and the score remained unchanged until late on when Roy Aitken charged into the box and was brought down to earn a penalty kick. Mo Johnston converted and despite the Swedes pulling one back, Scotland had done enough to earn a vital two points.

TUESDAY 16TH JUNE 1998

Exactly 80 years to the day since the Swedish victory, Scotland again stood on the World Cup brink against Scandinavians as they faced Norway in Bordeaux. It seemed a must-win clash for both sides as Scotland had lost their opener to Brazil while Norway had managed only a draw with Morocco and were up against the tournament favourites next. Scotland were the better team throughout but having conceded the opening goal against the run of play, it needed an equaliser from Craig Burley to ensure a share of the spoils. Everyone in the group would have something to play for going into the final round of fixtures.

SATURDAY 17TH JUNE 1989

The Scotland kids playing at the under-17 World Cup headed north for their quarter-final when they took on East Germany at Pittodrie. The match seemed destined for extra time. In injury time John Lindsay scored the winner for the hosts and the eyes of the nation turned towards Tynecastle for the semi-final against Portugal.

TUESDAY 18TH JUNE 1974

Scotland moved to Frankfurt for their second game at the 1974 World Cup finals and more than matched the might of world champions Brazil in a 0-0 draw. Brazil were not as strong as four years previously but it was still a significant performance as the Scots showed themselves more than capable of playing on the big stage. A draw was probably fair overall but Scotland had chances to win and Billy Bremner instinctively sticking out a leg to deflect a rebound inches the wrong side of the post, remains one of the country's greatest 'if only' moments.

FRIDAY 18TH JUNE 1982

If Brazil were on the way down in 1974, they had bounced back by 1982 when they hammered Scotland in the heat of Seville. Despite taking the lead through Dave Narey, Scotland were treated to a lesson as Brazil, inspired by Zico, eventually ran out 4-1 winners. The heavy defeat matched Scotland's margin of victory against New Zealand and reduced their goal difference back to zero so a win would be needed against the Soviet Union in the final game to progress.

THURSDAY 18TH JUNE 1992

The Euro 92 campaign finished on a high despite losses to Holland and Germany as the Commonwealth of Independent States (formerly the Soviet Union) were defeated 3-0 in Norrköping. Paul McStay, Brian McClair and Gary McAllister grabbed the goals.

TUESDAY 18TH JUNE 1996

Scotland defeated Switzerland 1-0 on a nervous night in Birmingham but yet again goal difference would knock the team out of a major championship. Ally McCoist scored but it was not enough as Patrick Kluivert's late strike against England at Wembley was enough to send the Dutch through, despite a 4-1 defeat, and Scotland home.

SATURDAY 19TH JUNE 1954

The shambolic World Cup campaign of 1954 ended in a 7-0 humiliation against Uruguay in Basel. A hat-trick from Carlos Borges helped inflict Scotland's heaviest-ever defeat as the players melted under the hot Swiss sun.

TUESDAY 20th JUNE 1989

World Cup fever had caught on in Scotland and an astonishing crowd of 28,555 squeezed into Tynecastle to watch the under-17 semi-final with Portugal. Another 1-0 success took Scotland to the final with Brian O'Neill scoring the goal.

WEDNESDAY 20th JUNE 1990

Scotland looked to progress to the second round of the World Cup in 1990 with a draw, or better, against Brazil. It was goalless until late on when Müller tapped home a rebound from an acute angle and Taffarel's point-blank save in the final seconds meant the game had slipped away. All was not lost though as one of the best third-place spots could still be claimed, depending on the score in the match between South Korea and Uruguay the next day.

THURSDAY 21st JUNE 1990

After the disappointment of the Brazil defeat, Scotland looked to Udinese where Uruguay would play South Korea. A draw or narrow Korea win would keep Scotland alive but a dire game, practically without highlight, was decided deep into injury time when the South American villains from 1986 scored from a free kick. The draw alone would not have been enough for Scotland as they had an identical record to Austria meaning lots would be drawn to decide who progressed.

SATURDAY 22nd JUNE 1974

Scotland realistically had to defeat Yugoslavia to reach the second round in 1974. Joe Jordan scored a last-minute equaliser in a 1-1 draw but Brazil later defeated Zaire 3-0 to send Scotland out by a solitary goal.

TUESDAY 22nd JUNE 1982

Scotland were knocked out of the World Cup on goal difference for the third successive time following a 2-2 draw with the Soviet Union. Despite Joe Jordan's opener the Soviets equalised and then took the lead in comical fashion when Alan Hansen and Willie Miller ran into each other. Graeme Souness secured a draw but another fine Scotland side was heading home having failed to progress beyond the first round.

FRIDAY 23RD JUNE 1972

A Scotland party of 29 players, coaches and officials left Glasgow to take part in the Brazilian Independence Cup. The journey began with a flight to Gatwick before a quick switch to Heathrow for an onward plane to Paris and a final connecting flight to take the squad to Rio. Manager Tommy Docherty was reportedly unhappy that details of the players' bonus had been leaked with each man set to pocket £500 if they reached the final.

TUESDAY 23RD JUNE 1998

Scotland faced Morocco in the final World Cup group game in St Etienne knowing a win was needed to have a chance of staying in the tournament. Sadly, the clinical Moroccans made the most of their chances to record a convincing 3-0 win which also saw Craig Burley sent off. However, the Moroccans were still knocked out as Norway defeated Brazil elsewhere.

WEDNESDAY 24TH JUNE 1314

Scotland recorded a significant home win over England in 1314 when the armies of Robert the Bruce triumphed on this day in the Battle of Bannockburn. This victory is now recalled before every international game in the form of the song Flower Of Scotland which has become firmly established as the pre-match anthem.

SATURDAY 24TH JUNE 1989

Over 50,000 people basked in the Hampden sun as Scotland took on Saudi Arabia in the under-17 World Cup final. Coach Craig Brown and players such as future full internationals Andy McLaren, Paul Dickov and Brian O'Neill were defeated as the Saudis won 5-4 on penalties following a 2-2 draw. *The Evening Times* commented that the Saudis were 'all moustached and maturity' and though Fifa had to take passport evidence on face value, suspicion remains in Scotland.

TUESDAY 25TH JUNE 1974

Despite the first-round exit, the World Cup squad of 1974 arrived back at Glasgow Airport to a heroes' welcome as 10,000 fans waited to greet them. Sir William Gray, Lord Provost of Glasgow, wrote to the team congratulating them on their efforts.

THURSDAY 26TH JUNE 1952

Popular Scottish defender Gordon McQueen was born on this day in Kilwinning. Though he started senior football with St Mirren he would make his name south of the border with both Leeds and Manchester United. He would earn 30 caps in total with one of the highlights being the opening goal in the 2-1 defeat of England at Wembley in 1977. Unfortunately, injury ruled him out of the 1978 World Cup and several commentators believe he would have made a difference. Along with spells coaching and managing after playing he also became involved with the media and his televised reaction to Scotland goals during the Euro 2008 campaign endeared him to the fans once more.

SATURDAY 26TH JUNE 1982

Actor John Gordon Sinclair, who came to fame in the film *Gregory's Girl*, teamed up with the Scottish World Cup squad to record We Have a Dream. The exit from the World Cup finals also spelled the end for the official song and it exited the charts on this day in 1982. Compared to some of the monstrosities produced – in fairness not just by Scotland – it was one of the better efforts of its type and was also re-released in 2008 as a charity single with several Scottish celebrities, and a recording of the Tartan Army, featuring on the track.

THURSDAY 27TH JUNE 1974

It was not only the people of Scotland who felt proud of the team for their performances at the 1974 World Cup, the Tennent's Caledonian Brewery was also happy with what it had seen. Irrespective of the first-round exit, it announced the bonus payment it would make to the squad would be increased from £7,500 to £10,000.

MONDAY 28TH JUNE 1954

While the World Cup is now the undisputed highlight of the football calendar, it was not always thus. Violence following the tie between Hungary and Brazil moved Robert Kelly, chairman of Celtic and president of the Scottish Football League, to state: "I can say that no Celtic player will ever be asked to take part in the competition again."

THURSDAY 29TH JUNE 1950

While most Scots content themselves with a sly grin at the thought of England's infamous 1-0 defeat to the USA in Belo Horizonte, two had a much better reason to celebrate properly. Edinburgh-born Bill Jeffrey was the American manager on that day while Eddie McIlveney, born in Greenock, had been fast-tracked into the side following his recent immigration to the country.

THURSDAY 29TH JUNE 1972

Scotland played in the city of Belo Horizonte 22 years after England had been humbled in the same location. Scotland's first match in the Brazilian Independence Cup was against Yugoslavia and they fared far better than those from south of the border, as a double from Lou Macari was enough to secure a 2-2 draw.

FRIDAY 29TH JUNE 1973

The SFA hosted a banquet at the city chambers in Glasgow to celebrate its 100th anniversary. Over 40 countries from the football world were represented.

SATURDAY 30TH JUNE 1973

While the morning after the night before may not have been so pleasant, the SFA centenary celebrations continued in the afternoon as Scotland hosted Brazil in a glamorous friendly. Cynics may suggest that the outcome – a lot of huffing and puffing during an honourable defeat – was appropriate to the occasion as Brazil won 1-0.

MONDAY 30TH JUNE 1986

The reign of Alex Ferguson as Scotland manager was officially over at the end of the month. Ferguson had taken over from Jock Stein in the previous autumn and though he had guided the team to the World Cup finals, a tough group had resulted in first-round elimination once more. His career was still taking off as his excellent record with Aberdeen persuaded Manchester United he was the man to turn things round at Old Trafford. He did just that and with a total of more than 30 years of success, including several league titles and four major European triumphs, he is one of the finest Scottish managers of all time.

SCOTLAND
On This Day

JULY

MONDAY 1st JULY 1940

Craig Brown, one of Scotland's most successful managers, was born on this day. As a player he had a very modest career which was severely hampered by injury, although he was part of the Dundee squad which won the championship in 1962. It was as a coach that he really excelled, starting with Motherwell as an assistant in 1974 before becoming the manager of Clyde and leading them into the Premier Division. The SFA soon moved to take him into the national set-up and after working with the youth teams he was appointed Scotland manager following the departure of Andy Roxburgh in 1993. While Scotland manager, Brown was sometimes criticised for a defensive style and a reliance on older players but it is undeniable he produced excellent results to reach the finals of both Euro 96 and the 1998 World Cup. A disappointing campaign preceding the 2002 World Cup saw him leave his post with a record of 32 wins and only 20 losses from 70 matches.

WEDNESDAY 2nd JULY 1930

The first of two Tommy Gemmells to play for Scotland was born in 1930 in Tarbolton. Gemmell's only club in senior football was St Mirren and he was capped twice, against Portugal and Yugoslavia, in 1955. He managed a goal in his first game but despite this impressive feat he was not picked again.

SUNDAY 2nd JULY 1972

After facing Yugoslavia in Belo Horizonte, Porto Alegre hosted Scotland's second game of the Brazilian Independence Cup when they took on Czechoslovakia. With world champions and tournament hosts Brazil awaiting Scotland in the final match, the side really needed a win here to have a chance of progressing but could manage only a 0-0 draw.

TUESDAY 3rd JULY 2001

Billy Liddell, one of Scotland's finest post-war players, died in 2001. He was a key component in the Liverpool team that won the championship in 1947 and though that side deteriorated, he showed admirable loyalty and continued to play with distinction. Between 1947 and 1955 he made nearly 30 appearances for Scotland, scoring six times.

SUNDAY 4TH JULY 2010

Scotland's recent failure to reach the finals of major tournaments has resulted in some members of the Tartan Army looking closer to home for holiday destinations. Gatherings in Aviemore have proved popular with families and on this day fans were entertained by events such as the Kilted five-a-side World Cup and the Kilted keepie-uppie competition.

TUESDAY 5TH JULY 1960

Gary Gillespie, holder of 13 international caps, was born on this day in Bonnybridge. He showed potential as a young player with Falkirk before he moved to England where he enjoyed success with Coventry and Liverpool. Initially he appeared to be a lucky mascot for Scotland as his first six national games brought five wins and a draw but injuries took their toll and probably stopped him fulfilling his true potential. He appeared in one game at the 1990 World Cup finals, against Brazil.

WEDNESDAY 5TH JULY 1972

Scotland faced Brazil in the final group game of the Brazilian Independence Cup knowing they needed at least a draw to have a chance of reaching the knockout stages of the competition. Despite a valiant effort, particularly from goalkeeper Bobby Clark, Scotland went down to a late goal in front of 130,000 people in Rio, the largest attendance at any Scotland away game. The defeat eliminated Scotland from the tournament as either Yugoslavia or Czechoslovakia would definitely move above them after the final game which would be played the next day.

WEDNESDAY 6TH JULY 2005

Scottish football usually has very limited interest in the Olympics but this was not the case when London won the bidding process to host the games in 2012. Hampden Park had been nominated as one of the grounds capable of holding the football competition but not everyone was relishing the prospect of Scottish involvement. Despite it becoming apparent Team GB would enter the football in some form, the SFA would immediately stress that it would not be putting forward players for the cause. It was believed that Team GB would pose a serious threat to the future of Scotland as an independent football nation.

MONDAY 7TH JULY 1975

SFA president Rankin Grimshaw clarified remarks he had made questioning the ability of manager Willie Ormond following a draw with Romania. He had suggested another manager may get more out of the players but insisted this was his own personal view and not the position of the SFA. With such feeble backing from his bosses, it was no surprise Ormond departed later in the year.

FRIDAY 7TH JULY 1978

The inquest into the World Cup debacle began with a meeting of the SFA international committee. A full and frank exchange of views preceded a vote on whether manager Ally MacLeod should keep his job and by the casting vote of the chairman he survived. However, it was soon clear that this vote of confidence was only a temporary measure and MacLeod would depart after leading the team for just one more game.

MONDAY 8TH JULY 1878

Future Celtic and Scotland striker Jimmy Quinn was born on this day. Quinn was incredibly successful, winning six championships and five Scottish cups while earning 11 Scotland caps. He scored seven goals for the national team with his most notable performance coming against Ireland in 1908, when he notched four.

TUESDAY 9TH JULY 1867

On this day in 1867 a group of men met to found Queen's Park. They would provide the entire Scotland side for the first international against England and supplied a total of 80 players who earned caps. To date, only Rangers and Celtic have produced more internationals although Hearts join this group. Queen's Park were also responsible for building Hampden Park, still the home of Scottish football more than a century after its construction.

THURSDAY 9TH JULY 2009

The SFA were dealt a blow by the news that Diadora's UK operation had gone into liquidation. The kit supplier to the Scotland national team had at least provided enough equipment to ensure there was no shortage for the final qualifying games in the 2010 World Cup campaign.

MONDAY 10TH JULY 1978

The SFA announced that the Scotland under-21 side would take on the USA in September. It was thought that the new group of players were in need of match practice and they made the most of this chance to take to the field by winning 3-1.

MONDAY 10TH JULY 1989

Maurice Johnston caused one of the biggest shocks in Scottish football by signing for Rangers. Though not the first Catholic to play for Rangers, he was one of the most prominent and the nature of his transfer – having been photographed preparing to return to Celtic from French club Nantes – sparked a tabloid frenzy. Johnston had been in excellent form for Scotland, scoring six goals in the qualifiers for Italia 90.

THURSDAY 11TH JULY 1872

One-cap wonder Matthew Scott was born on this day. He captained the side to a convincing 5-2 victory over Wales in 1898 in his only appearance but was never selected again.

THURSDAY 12TH JULY 1962

Manchester United splashed out a record £115,000 to sign Denis Law from Torino. Law's time in Italy was not completely happy and after a dispute with the management he was eventually transferred back to England. Though he did not play in the 1968 European Cup win due to injury, he was a key player in Matt Busby's second great team which won two league championships and an FA Cup. During this time he was established as Scotland's main striker and scored a record 30 goals in 55 international appearances.

MONDAY 12TH JULY 1982

England and Scotland held a private meeting at the Fifa congress to discuss the forthcoming fixture at Wembley in 1983. The hosts suggested playing on a Tuesday to avoid clashing with a holiday weekend and the SFA agreed, providing Scotland were given an official allocation of tickets once more. The FA had, very unsuccessfully, attempted to ban Scottish fans from previous games in London but this policy was set to end.

SUNDAY 13th JULY 1924

George Farm was born on this day in Edinburgh. He collected ten caps over a period of several years in the 1950s but upon retiring from the game, he took up one of the more unusual occupations for ex-footballers. As well as working as a commentator for a local radio station, he also held a position as a lighthouse keeper.

SUNDAY 14th JULY 1957

Scotland international full-back Arthur Albiston was born in Edinburgh on this day. He made his debut for Manchester United in a city derby and showed his appetite for the big occasion by winning the FA Cup while still in his teens. Though he was capped only 14 times, he made himself a regular in the team during the 1980s and played against Uruguay in the 1986 World Cup finals.

THURSDAY 15th JULY 1993

A record was set for a transfer fee between two Scottish clubs when Rangers paid Dundee United £3.7m for Scotland striker Duncan Ferguson. Clauses in the deal could have increased the fee to over £4m depending on future appearances for Scotland. Ferguson had already missed an important World Cup qualifier in Lisbon after breaking a toe in an alleged bar brawl and his international career failed to take off.

WEDNESDAY 16th JULY 1986

Scotland made a shock appointment by installing Andy Roxburgh as manager to replace Alex Ferguson, who had led the team in Mexico. With Ferguson acting as a stand-in following the death of Jock Stein the previous year, it was always known a new manager would be needed but few in the game expected someone to be handed the position without experience of club management. However, Roxburgh was a talented coach with plenty of international experience through working with the youth teams. He successfully guided the side to the World Cup finals in 1990 and, for the first time ever, to the finals of the European Championships in 1992. His time was not without difficulties as some players seemed to grudge him respect and he resigned after a disappointing campaign in the 1994 World Cup qualifiers.

WEDNESDAY 17TH JULY 1946

Peter Cormack was born in Granton. The midfielder was capped only nine times for Scotland but has the rare distinction of earning his caps under five different managers. He made his debut in a Hampden Park draw with a Brazil side containing Pele, but despite his determined displays he did not manage to secure a regular place in the team. Another eight caps were added to his collection over the years but his best achievements came at club level, winning two league championships, the FA Cup and the Uefa Cup with Liverpool.

MONDAY 17TH JULY 1995

Former Scotland player George Graham had been banned from football for a year by the FA for his part in a bung scandal as manager of Arsenal and world governing body Fifa endorsed that, on this day. Graham would later return to management with Leeds United and Spurs but though he guided the former to Europe and won the League Cup for the latter, he could not recreate his glory days at Highbury and has not returned to football since being sacked from White Hart Lane. He developed a successful media career after leaving Spurs.

TUESDAY 18TH JULY 2006

The Scotland under-19 side kicked off their campaign at the European Championship finals in Poland with a 2-2 draw against Portugal. The youngsters would have been disappointed to let a two-goal lead slip in the last 20 minutes and the games with Turkey and Spain would decide whether or not they would progress to the semi-finals. They had reached the finals by making it through two qualification groups. In the latter, they knocked out France in a mini-tournament held in Belarus.

TUESDAY 19TH JULY 1977

The SFA decided to lift the life bans which had been imposed on the Copenhagen five. New manager Ally MacLeod had said he wanted everyone available for selection, though the SFA stressed the reprieves had not been granted because of his views. However, despite the slate being wiped clean for everyone, only Arthur Graham and Joe Harper would be picked again for Scotland.

THURSDAY 20TH JULY 1978

England under-21 international Nigel Quashie was born in London on this day. However, as well as collecting England caps at youth level, he is also the owner of 14 full Scotland caps as he switched allegiance in 2004. He was eligible to play for Scotland since his grandfather was born in Glasgow. Despite being brought up south of the border, he was always a fully committed player in the dark blue. He found the net once for his adopted country but despite starting in the Euro 2008 qualifiers he drifted out of contention late in 2007. Quashie also holds the distinction of being the first black player to represent Scotland in over 120 years.

TUESDAY 21ST JULY 1964

One of Scotland's most skilful footballers of the 1960s, John White, was killed on this day. White had been sheltering under a tree on a golf course which was struck by lightning during a storm. He had started his career in Scotland with Alloa and Falkirk but soon moved south to join Spurs. He was an immense success at White Hart Lane, winning the double in 1961, the FA Cup in 1962 and the Cup Winners' Cup in 1963. For Scotland, the inside-forward had already collected 22 caps, scoring three times, and was part of the side which missed out on a place at the 1962 World Cup finals by losing a play-off to eventual runners-up Czechoslovakia. He died aged 27 and, still in the prime of his football career, it is almost universally agreed he would have achieved even more success in the game with both club and country.

TUESDAY 21ST JULY 1981

East Stirlingshire confirmed that Scotland legend Jim Baxter had applied to be their manager. Unfortunately for Baxter, the club turned down his offer and he remained out of football following his retirement from the game several years earlier. Baxter ran a pub when his playing days were over, a decidedly questionable choice for someone with his problems with alcohol. He required a double liver transplant and six years later, in 2001, was diagnosed with pancreatic cancer. A few months later he lost his life to the disease, aged 61.

NIGEL QUASHIE WAS BORN SOUTH OF THE BORDER BUT WAS ELIGIBLE TO PLAY FOR SCOTLAND.

TUESDAY 22ND JULY 2003

Renowned football journalist Alex Cameron died on this day. 'Candid' Cameron was a dedicated reporter and columnist for both newspaper and television but despite numerous scoops over the years, he is best remembered for a more unfortunate incident in 1977. While previewing Scotland against Czechoslovakia outside Hampden, Cameron found himself rudely shoved from behind. The barrage from his assailant continued despite Cameron's anger but that subsided into shock when he discovered he was being jostled by a police horse, which succeeded in moving him several yards!

SUNDAY 23RD JULY 2006

Scotland under-19s reached the semi-finals of the European Championships by defeating Turkey 3-2. The win was enough to take the young Scots through as runners-up as Portugal were held to a draw in their final game with group winners Spain, leaving them a point behind in third place. Scotland seemed to be home and dry in this contest as they stormed into a three-goal lead by the hour mark but two Turkish goals ensured a nervous finish to the game.

THURSDAY 24TH JULY 1958

Jim Leighton was born on this day in Johnstone. He started his career with the great Aberdeen side of the 1980s which earned him several medals including the European Cup Winners' Cup of 1983. He then moved to Manchester United with Alex Ferguson. Though he initially played well at Old Trafford, flaws emerged in his game and after a disastrous FA Cup Final in 1990 he was dropped, effectively for good. He returned to Scotland with a battered reputation but gradually regained his confidence with Dundee, Hibs and then finally Aberdeen. His form recovered to the extent that he was good enough for Scotland once more and his battles with Andy Goram for the number-one jersey in the mid-1990s became legendary. Leighton missed out on Euro 96 but did have the starting berth for the World Cup finals in 1998. Sadly, his career ended on low notes with a poor performance for Scotland leading him to retire from the national team, while his last competitive game for Aberdeen ended after only a few minutes when he was injured in the Scottish Cup Final of 2000.

SATURDAY 25TH JULY 1925

The magnificently named Harry Haddock was born in Glasgow on this day. World War II interfered with the start of his football career but after impressing in the juniors after peace returned, he signed for Clyde and continued to improve. With the Bully Wee he won two Scottish Cups, captaining the side in the second triumph against Hibs, and collected six Scotland caps. He played against the great Puskas-inspired Hungary team on his debut in 1954 but a loss in that game would set the tone for his Scotland career. In a further five appearances he would taste victory only once, against Portugal, but he lost a further three times including twice against England. The first of these was a particularly bitter pill to swallow in the form of a 7-2 hammering.

SATURDAY 26TH JULY 1930

A Scot scored in the World Cup for the first time on this day when Jim Brown found the net against Argentina. Despite being born in Kilmarnock, he was playing for America – who had reached the semi-finals of the first tournament – but they were blown away by their opponents who claimed a comprehensive 6-1 victory. Brown's goal, scored in front of 80,000 fans in Montevideo, was a consolation bagged in the closing stages but Argentina slumped to defeat in the final against hosts Uruguay. Brown was not the last Scottish player to feature for the USA side over the years as they frequently made the most of immigrants who had come to their country to shore up a side which initially lacked native talent. Sadly, there is still a strong case to be made for his semi-final goal making him the most successful Scottish World Cup player of all time!

WEDNESDAY 26TH JULY 2006

Scotland reached their first major representative final in 24 years when the under-19s defeated the Czech Republic 1-0 in the 2006 European Championships. Calum Elliot scored the only goal of the game early in the second half to carry Scotland into the final which would be against Spain. Having already lost 4-0 to the Spanish in the group phase, the odds were stacked against the young Scots ahead of the final.

TUESDAY 27th JULY 1971

Bobby Brown, the manager who led Scotland to the famous Wembley triumph of 1967, was sacked on this day in 1971. Brown had made the perfect start in charge of the side by defeating England, but that win was not enough to progress to the knockout stages of the 1968 European Championships. The side then missed out in qualifying for the 1970 World Cup – albeit knocked out by West Germany, runners-up in 1966 and semi-finalists in Mexico – and after successive away losses to Belgium, Portugal and Denmark, with one goal in the three games, Brown departed. His time at the cutting edge in football was effectively over as although he did some work for Plymouth Argyle, he began to concentrate on interests outside of the game.

TUESDAY 28th JULY 1970

Scotland international Billy Bremner committed his future to Leeds United by signing a new four-year contract. At this time Elland Road was like a Scottish international colony as Bremner was joined by Peter Lorimer, Gordon McQueen, Frank and Eddie Gray, Joe Jordan, Arthur Graham, David Stewart and David Harvey at various points throughout the decade. Though the Scottish presence in Leeds has declined over the years, both Gary McAllister and Gordon Strachan spent significant parts of their careers there while the club also provided further Scottish internationals in the form of David Hopkin and Dominic Matteo.

THURSDAY 28th JULY 1994

Former Scotland player Hugh Brown died on this day. Brown was a powerful midfielder who made his name at Partick Thistle as World War II came to an end and he helped the Jags win the Summer Cup. His performances continued to impress as the regular habit of peacetime football returned to Scotland. Brown was selected for Scotland in defeats against Wales and Belgium before tasting victory in his last international appearance against Luxembourg. He moved south from Partick Thistle but rather than going to a club in the top flight as was common for Scottish players at the time, he joined Torquay United who were in the Third Division. His time in the game was coming to an end though and he hung up his boots upon leaving Plainmoor.

WEDNESDAY 29TH JULY 1970

The SFA discussed the possibility of moving the November home match against Denmark from Glasgow. It was feared that the city would be too congested at that time of year but eventually it was decided to carry on as normal. A crowd of only 24,618 turned up on the Hampden Park terraces to see Scotland defeat the Danes 1-0.

SATURDAY 29TH JULY 2006

The Scotland under-19 side produced a brave display against Spain in the final of the 2006 European Championships but still lost 2-1. The young Scots were given hope by Graham Dorrans scoring late in the game but they could not force an equaliser having trailed by two, and it turned out to be only a consolation. However, the value of such tournaments should not be underestimated as players such as Lee Wallace, Steven Fletcher and Graham Dorrans all picked up international experience which helped them en route to the full Scotland squad. The Spain side which won the competition contained future full internationals Gerard Pique, Juan Mata and Diego Capel.

SUNDAY 29TH JULY 2007

The *Scotland on Sunday* reported that former SFA secretary Jim Farry had been given a position working as a business development manager for a commercial interiors company. Farry had been sacked from his job at the SFA in 1999 after it was deemed he had deliberately held up the registration of Jorge Cadete, delaying his availability for Celtic games. Before this incident Farry had been a prominent figure in Scottish football and played an important role in the redevelopment of Hampden Park. He was also credited for his tough stance when negotiating the order in which the national team would play qualifying fixtures. He had not played football at a high level but after joining the Scottish Football League in the 1970s showed himself to be an able administrator by moving up in the organisation to hold the position of secretary before switching to the SFA in 1990. The Cadete affair was not his first brush with controversy as he was somewhat harshly criticised for his attempts to prevent the Scotland match with Belarus being rescheduled when it clashed with the funeral of Princess Diana in 1997.

TUESDAY 30th JULY 1946

Prolific striker John Deans was born in Linwood. His astonishing scoring record for junior side Neilston earned him the nickname of Dixie, in honour of the legendary Everton striker of the same name, and he set about making a huge impact on Scottish football. Motherwell won the race for his signature when he entered the senior game but despite delivering plenty of goals at Fir Park, he developed disciplinary problems and collected several red cards. Celtic signed him for a bargain price in 1971 and the goals continued to flow. Unfortunately, he became infamous for missing the only penalty in Celtic's shoot-out loss to Inter Milan in the 1974 European Cup semi-final. However, that did not stop him earning international recognition shortly afterwards when he was capped against East Germany and Spain. By this stage, his scoring powers were on the wane and he moved down south to play for Luton Town and Carlisle United before rediscovering the goal touch in Australia for Adelaide City. He returned to Scotland to play with Partick Thistle before retiring.

WEDNESDAY 31st JULY 1974

The SFA council agreed with manager Willie Ormond that there was a need to play more friendly games. It was decided to try to arrange an international challenge match at Hampden Park for the end of October.

MONDAY 31st JULY 1967

Scotland midfielder Derek Ferguson was born on this day in Glasgow. As a talented youngster he earned caps at youth level and played for Rangers during their initial success under Graeme Souness in the 1980s. Excellent control and superb passing ability seemed to mark Ferguson out for a big future in the game but injury problems and some issues off the park harmed his chances. He earned two full caps while at Ibrox, against Malta and Colombia, before he moved on to Hearts in 1990. After a few seasons at Tynecastle he went south to join Sunderland but though he made a contribution on Wearside, there was the lingering feeling of 'what if' about his career. He is the older brother of Barry Ferguson, who continued the family football tradition by playing for Rangers and Scotland as well as for clubs in England.

SCOTLAND
On This Day

AUGUST

SUNDAY 1st AUGUST 1943

Andy Roxburgh was born on this day in Glasgow. Roxburgh began his playing career with the amateurs of Queen's Park in 1961 before moving on to East Stirlingshire, Partick Thistle, Falkirk and Clydebank, scoring nearly 80 goals in over 200 league games. After retiring as a player, he quickly embarked on the course which would take him to the office of national team manager. He spent several years coaching Scotland's under-16, under-18 and under-21 sides before taking the senior job in 1986. Scotland qualified for the World Cup in 1990 and Euro 92 under his stewardship before he resigned following the failure to qualify for the 1994 World Cup. Roxburgh's qualities were recognised by European governing body Uefa who made him technical director in 1994 after he left the SFA.

FRIDAY 2nd AUGUST 2002

When Dennis Wise was sacked by Leicester City in 2002, Scotland international Callum Davidson had reason for a wry smile. Wise was dismissed after being sent home from a pre-season tour of Finland when a dispute over a game of cards escalated to violence, leaving the unfortunate Davidson with a double fracture of his jaw. He had joined Leicester two years before the incident and was a regular in the Scotland squad at this time. He had started his career with St Johnstone before moving south to join Blackburn Rovers, and from Ewood Park he moved to Leicester for £1.75m. After earning his 17th cap in 2002, he had to wait seven years before being picked again, when George Burley recalled him for the ill-fated 4-0 defeat in Norway and the Hampden victory over Macedonia. By this time he was with Preston North End, whom he had joined on a free transfer.

THURSDAY 3rd AUGUST 2006

Scotland fans at home who wanted to watch the first away game in the Euro 2008 qualifying campaign against Lithuania were given a good excuse to leave work early when the kick-off time was announced as 5.30pm. The early start meant the game could be accommodated on television as part of a double header which would also feature England's trip to Macedonia. The SFA estimated that over 3,000 fans would follow the team to Kaunas for the match.

SUNDAY 4TH AUGUST 1957

Scotland striker John Wark was born on this day. He earned 29 caps in the late 1970s and 1980s, scoring seven goals. The highlight of his Scotland career was to play all three games at the 1982 World Cup finals, where he scored twice against New Zealand. However, he also netted at Wembley in the 3-1 defeat of 1979.

TUESDAY 4TH AUGUST 2009

The squad George Burley named for the crunch World Cup qualifier with Norway in Oslo was a family affair as Burnley's Steven Caldwell was recalled to join brother Gary, who played with Celtic. Gary had established himself as a regular in the side and enjoyed a tremendous high when he scored the winning goal against France in 2006. His trip to Norway was one he would have wanted to forget, though, as he was sent off in the first half. Scotland crashed to a horrific 4-0 defeat. Steven made his first Scotland appearance in over three years in Oslo, earning his tenth cap.

THURSDAY 5TH AUGUST 1965

Future Scotland striker Joe McBride was transferred from Motherwell to Celtic on this day. He had a superb scoring record with the Fir Park club and with Celtic he continued to find the net at a remarkable rate. This earned him a call-up to the national squad but though he played against Wales and Northern Ireland in 1966, he failed to find the net. An injury ruled him out of the Celtic side as they were about to make history in Lisbon and although he scored often at Hibs after moving, he failed to regain his place in the Scotland team.

TUESDAY 6TH AUGUST 2002

Scotland fans in the capital were given a boost when Scotland manager Berti Vogts announced the side would return to Edinburgh for the first time in four years. The team would take on Canada in an Easter Road friendly and Vogts insisted he would use as many free international dates as possible to help give his young squad the experience they needed to reach the finals of major tournaments.

THURSDAY 7th AUGUST 1969

Paul Lambert was born in Paisley on this day. He would start his career with local club St Mirren, where he won the Scottish Cup, but it was with Motherwell that he moved into the international scene. The 1995 Kirin Cup saw Scotland use a number of players who were hoping to break into the squad on a regular basis but while some failed to do so, Lambert grabbed his chance and earned a total of 40 caps.

SATURDAY 7th AUGUST 2004

Gordon Smith, of Hibs' Famous Five fame, died. Smith earned 19 caps for Scotland, scoring four goals, and enjoyed huge success with Hibs. However, as well as winning the championship at Easter Road, he achieved the same feat with Hearts and Dundee, making him the only player to win the title with three different clubs.

MONDAY 8th AUGUST 1977

A scramble was expected as tickets for Scotland's World Cup qualifier against Czechoslovakia at Hampden went on sale. It was known a home win would put Scotland in pole position to reach the finals in Argentina and fans were able to buy tickets ranging from £1 for uncovered terracing to £6 for the main stand.

WEDNESDAY 8th AUGUST 1984

Gordon Strachan announced he would move south from Aberdeen to join Manchester United for a fee of £500,000. Strachan had enjoyed exceptional success in the north-east and would collect further honours south of the border. However, this transfer was not without controversy as the German club FC Cologne claimed Strachan had already promised to sign for them.

WEDNESDAY 8th AUGUST 2007

Sunderland confirmed that Scotland goalkeeper Craig Gordon would join them from Hearts after news of the transfer started to leak the previous night. The upfront fee received by the Gorgie club was £7m but further clauses meant the final figure could reach as high as £10m, an amount which would make Gordon by far the most expensive Scottish player ever.

FRIDAY 9TH AUGUST 1996

Paul Lambert enjoyed a belated birthday present when he signed for German giants Borussia Dortmund. The Scotland international had used the recent Bosman ruling to leave Motherwell on a free transfer but eyebrows were raised when Dortmund, one of the most ambitious clubs in Europe, took a chance on him. However, the coaches in Germany soon realised that while Lambert had been viewed mainly as an attacking player in Scotland, the qualities he possessed were better suited to a deeper role in the midfield. He developed into one of the most accomplished midfielders in Europe, anchoring Borussia to a Champions League victory in 1997 when they defeated Juventus 3-1 in Munich. Lambert's talents were also appreciated in the national team. He appeared in the 1998 World Cup finals, collected a total of 40 caps, and scored his only goal against the Faroe Islands in 2002.

TUESDAY 9TH AUGUST 2005

Walter Smith named his squad for an away friendly against Austria on this day but chose to restrict his options. With several Scotland players featuring for their clubs in European qualifiers at this crowded part of the season, Smith elected not to call up anyone from Rangers, Dundee United, Everton or Manchester United. Leaving out several established players gave those on the fringes of the squad a chance to impress and stake a claim for a more regular place. The squad contained 13 players, in the travelling party of 20, who had been capped ten times or less.

SATURDAY 10TH AUGUST 1974

An infamous Charity Shield clash took place at Wembley between Liverpool and Leeds United. There was a large Scottish presence on display as Liverpool, coached by Bill Shankly, had Peter Cormack in their side while Leeds named Billy Bremner, Gordon McQueen, Joe Jordan, Peter Lorimer and Eddie Gray in their starting line-up. The match finished in a 1-1 draw before Liverpool won in a penalty shoot-out, but the play was completely overshadowed by Bremner and Kevin Keegan indulging in a fist fight which saw both players sent off. The players discarded their shirts on the long walk back to the tunnel and both were later handed long bans by the FA for the incident.

MONDAY 11TH AUGUST 1913

Scotland's first manager, Andy Beattie, was born in 1913. He took the position on a part-time basis in 1954 and led the team to the World Cup finals in Switzerland. However, the SFA retained considerable power over the team which left Beattie frustrated and feeling he could not do the job properly. After a 1-0 defeat to Austria in the first game of the finals, Beattie actually announced he would resign from his post before the Uruguay match, though he agreed to take charge for the final 90 minutes.

WEDNESDAY 11TH AUGUST 1965

Ralph Brand signed for Manchester City from Rangers on this day. Brand was a deadly striker with the Ibrox club and collected several titles in the years he spent in Glasgow. He proved to be equally reliable for the Scotland side and he averaged a goal every game in earning eight caps in the early 1960s. He had drifted out of the Scotland set-up, even before he moved south to Manchester, but despite City earning promotion in his first season the scoring touch seemed to have vanished. After returning to Scotland to play for Raith Rovers and Hamilton, he moved into management before leaving the game.

WEDNESDAY 12TH AUGUST 1970

The international selection committee met with national team manager Bobby Brown. Along with setting out his plans for the season ahead, Brown also explained what lessons could be learned from observing the 1970 World Cup finals.

WEDNESDAY 12TH AUGUST 2009

A dark day in Scotland's recent football history occurred when Norway dismantled the team 4-0 in Oslo in a crucial World Cup qualifier. With Holland winning the group comfortably, Scotland needed at least a point, if not all three, to keep their play-off hopes on track. However, despite making a reasonable start, the game went horribly wrong when Gary Caldwell was sent off and Norway scored with a deflected free kick. Things went from bad to worse and George Burley, heavily criticised for his team selection, was put under tremendous pressure going into the final two games.

SATURDAY 13TH AUGUST 1977

Billy McNeill was a colossus on the pitch for Celtic and Scotland and was eager to become just as successful as a manager. After a couple of months with Clyde in 1977, he was appointed Aberdeen boss in June and tasted victory in his first game in charge, against Rangers, on this day. The 3-1 victory set the tone for an excellent season in the north-east and Aberdeen finished the Premier League campaign as runners-up. McNeill moved back to his spiritual home, Celtic Park, in the summer and in four years as Celtic boss he won three championships and both domestic cups. At Manchester City he secured promotion and kept them in the top flight for a season but then struggled both at Maine Road and Aston Villa before returning to Celtic. He led Celtic to a double in 1988 but despite winning another Scottish Cup in 1989, Rangers were beginning to outspend their city rivals by some way and McNeill resigned in 1991. With the exception of a brief spell with Hibs, this was his last position in football.

TUESDAY 14TH AUGUST 1984

Wales caused a stir by pulling out of the under-21 European Championships and placing the blame at the door of the SFA. It was alleged that the abandonment of the British Home Championship, sparked by the withdrawal of Scotland and England, had damaged the Welsh finances to the extent they could no longer afford to compete at youth level. Their decision left the Scotland under-21 side short of games in the coming season as they were scheduled to face the Welsh twice.

SATURDAY 15TH AUGUST 1959

A Scottish football record was set by Ian St John in 1959 when he scored a hat-trick in just two-and-a-half minutes. Motherwell were taking on Hibs at Easter Road in a League Cup tie when the striker achieved the feat and this quick-fire burst allowed the visitors to triumph 3-1. The goals were three of more than 100 which St John scored for the Fir Park club and he had established himself as a regular striker for Scotland even before Liverpool paid big money to take him to Anfield in 1961.

WEDNESDAY 16TH AUGUST 1995

Scotland fans at Hampden endured a nervous wait of over an hour until Ally McCoist headed home the only goal of the game in a crucial victory over Greece. The three points put Scotland in a very strong position in the race to finish second in the group behind favourites Russia but with the worst two runners-up in qualifying having to go through a play-off, it was also crucial that victories were secured in the remaining games at home to Finland and San Marino.

TUESDAY 16TH AUGUST 2005

The Scotland under-21 side ended a winless streak of almost two years when they finally tasted victory again in Austria. The 3-1 result against Austria under-21s was slightly less convincing than it sounds as the hosts started well but a double from Craig Beattie, after Gregor Robertson opened the scoring, secured the win. Future full internationals Scott Brown, David Marshall, Christophe Berra, Steven Whittaker, David Clarkson, Shaun Maloney and Kevin Thomson also featured.

WEDNESDAY 17TH AUGUST 2005

Scotland claimed a respectable draw in the friendly with Austria but it was slightly frustrating to settle for 2-2 having led late in the game. A goalkeeping error from substitute Rab Douglas, and a tremendous long shot, allowed Austria back into the contest after goals from Kenny Miller and Garry O'Connor, his first for his country, had given Scotland a first-half lead. Miller would have been pleased to end a long scoring drought with Scotland and he scored three times in the next two games, important World Cup qualifiers against Italy and Norway.

FRIDAY 17TH AUGUST 2007

James Morrison received a boost as it was confirmed by Fifa that he was able to play for the senior Scotland side. It was believed that he would be eligible despite being English born and appearing for England at youth level as he could switch allegiance due to his grandparents being Scottish. Morrison had, as per the rules, officially switched his football nationality before he turned 21 but had an anxious wait to hear back from Fifa.

ALLY McCOIST PLAYED MORE THAN 60 TIMES FOR SCOTLAND, SCORING 19 GOALS.

MONDAY 18TH AUGUST 1975

Contrary to original plans, no Scotland squad was announced on this day for the forthcoming European Championship qualifier in Denmark. This would enable manager Willie Ormond to watch Birmingham City play Manchester United the following night. It was hoped that Ormond would be able to effect reconciliation with Martin Buchan, with whom he had reportedly fallen out previously. Buchan was included in the squad, and played in the game, so the relationship appeared to be patched up successfully.

THURSDAY 18TH AUGUST 1983

A number of recent Scotland players celebrate their birthday on this day but they have had little luck so far. Kris Boyd was born in 1983 but despite an impressive scoring record which saw him bag seven international goals, he struggled to retain the faith of managers when a system featuring a lone striker was adopted. He made himself unavailable for selection under George Burley but has since returned under Craig Levein. John Kennedy and Mark Burchill were also born on this day, both in 1980, but the latter failed to score in six appearances and the former effectively had his career ended by a horror tackle on his international debut.

WEDNESDAY 18TH AUGUST 2004

It is said that the definition of insanity is doing something over and over again while expecting a different result and the fans who turned up at Hampden for Scotland's 3-0 friendly defeat to Hungary must have been verging on certifiable. Berti Vogts' insistence on playing as many practice matches as possible was not bearing fruit and less than 16,000 were in attendance for this latest humiliation.

WEDNESDAY 19TH AUGUST 1992

Scotland international Gordon Durie had a miserable time as his side Spurs lost 2-0 to Coventry City. At one point during the game he won a free kick but was later pulled up and charged with feigning injury. In what seemed like a test case, he was eventually handed a three-game ban although very few governing bodies now take this kind of action, perhaps feeling that punishing every incident retrospectively would create a shortage of players!

MONDAY 20TH AUGUST 1917

One of the most courageous footballers ever to have pulled on the dark blue of Scotland, Jimmy Speirs, died on this day. He had volunteered to join the army, though he would have been exempt from conscription, in World War I and having already won a medal for bravery, he died in battle at Passchendaele. His football career had been ended by the conflict, with the last game in his professional career being for Bradford. The 1911 FA Cup provided his greatest success as he captained the Bantams to victory and even contributed the winning goal. He had moved south after playing for Clyde and Rangers and it was with the Ibrox club he earned his only Scotland cap, playing in the 1908 defeat of Wales.

WEDNESDAY 20TH AUGUST 2003

Scotland geared up for a number of important Euro 2004 qualifiers with a friendly game against Norway. This 0-0 draw in Oslo was rarely exciting but the side showed determination and organisation in defence which had been missing in previous away games. The last four trips had produced two defeats and a draw in the Faroe Islands! The Norwegian side were doing well in their qualification group and finished in the runners-up spot narrowly behind Denmark. However, their efforts in the play-offs would be similar to Scotland as, after a good first leg, they slumped to a heavy 5-1 aggregate defeat against Spain. This match was also notable for a young Darren Fletcher making his Scotland debut as a second-half substitute.

WEDNESDAY 20TH AUGUST 2008

George Burley's search for a first win as Scotland manager continued when Northern Ireland left Hampden with a 0-0 draw. This was his third match in charge but after a draw with Croatia, and defeat in the Czech Republic, he was yet to taste victory. Scotland dominated, though they found it hard to create chances, but needed an Allan McGregor penalty save, after the goalkeeper himself conceded the award, to avoid defeat. Burley's decision to leave Kris Boyd on the bench for 90 minutes to give his first-choice front line time to play together was an early indication of problems to come between the two men.

FRIDAY 21st AUGUST 1970

David Hopkin was born in Greenock on this day. Hopkin started his career with local club Morton before earning a big-money move to Chelsea in 1992 while still a youngster. However, at Stamford Bridge he failed to establish himself as a regular in the starting line-up despite frequently being in the matchday squad and he moved on to Crystal Palace. It was with the Selhurst Park club he excelled, with his dominating performances in midfield, and a stunning goal in a Wembley play-off final helping to take the Londoners to the Premiership. Hopkin's form earned him international recognition towards the end of the 1998 World Cup qualifying campaign, and the high point of his seven Scotland appearances came when he scored a double against Belarus.

WEDNESDAY 21st AUGUST 2002

Scotland's losing run under Berti Vogts continued with a 1-0 home defeat to Denmark. This latest setback meant the first five full international games of the German's reign had been lost as the one win, against a Hong Kong select, was not recognised by Fifa. Scotland had scored a mere two goals in the five losses.

SATURDAY 22nd AUGUST 1959

Davie Meiklejohn, one of the best players in Scotland before World War II, died on this day. The Rangers legend racked up over 600 appearances for the Ibrox club and he boasted one of the largest medal hauls in the game, winning 12 championships and four Scottish Cups, though he also tasted Hampden defeat on three occasions. Naturally, his form caught the eye of the international selectors and he made the first of 15 Scotland appearances against Wales in 1922. Despite his defensive position, he contributed three goals.

WEDNESDAY 22nd AUGUST 2007

Scotland took on South Africa for the second – and to date last – time in 2007. Having been beaten in the first meeting between the teams in 2002, Scotland gained some revenge by winning this contest 1-0 thanks to a late goal from Kris Boyd. The win maintained Scotland's momentum as they looked to conclude the Euro 2008 qualifiers on a high.

FRIDAY 23RD AUGUST 1963

Arsenal splashed the cash when they signed Ian Ure from Dundee for £62,500. This was a record fee for a player in his position. Though Ure enjoyed a good first season at Highbury, but injury and a loss of form meant he struggled to hold down a regular place in the team in future years. His Scotland career had ended with 11 appearances before he moved to Manchester United. The only honour collected in his career was the 1962 Scottish championship.

WEDNESDAY 23RD AUGUST 1972

Supporters of Scotland were able to breathe a little easier when Uruguay announced they would amend a proposal which would have forced the adoption of a Great Britain team for international competition. The Uruguayans pointed out they had no real objection to the Home Nations competing separately but they were unhappy that Scotland, England, Wales and Northern Ireland were all able to vote in the International Football Association Board. Fifa also holds four votes but with six needed to pass motions, the Home Nations retain a disproportionate amount of power, which frequently frustrates other associations across the world.

THURSDAY 24TH AUGUST 2000

Bob McPhail, one of the most prolific scorers in Scotland, died on this day aged 94. McPhail made an explosive start to his career with Airdrie and helped the Diamonds win the only major honour in their history, the 1924 Scottish Cup. His goals brought him a move to Rangers and as well as racking up title after title at Ibrox, he collected 17 international caps for Scotland, scoring seven times. Remarkably, his first four goals for Scotland all came against Ireland before he bagged a double against England in the Hampden victory of 1937, and a further goal against Czechoslovakia.

WEDNESDAY 25TH AUGUST 1971

Local magistrates made a tour of Glasgow's football grounds, including national stadium Hampden Park. They would not have been impressed with what they saw, a crumbling ground in dire need of renovation. With Queen's Park in desperate need of financial assistance, and money hard to raise from other sources, the future looked uncertain.

MONDAY 26TH AUGUST 1946

Don Masson was born on this day in Banchory. Masson spent the majority of his career in England, starting with Middlesbrough and Notts County before moving to QPR. He played in the lower leagues until his late 20s but eventually developed into a fine player, taking an important role for the Loftus Road side as they narrowly missed out on winning the First Division in 1976. It was in this year that Masson, just short of his 30th birthday, made his Scotland debut and he would later show nerves of steel to net a crucial World Cup penalty against Wales in 1977. However, it was suspected that by the time of the finals in Argentina he was past his best and he played only once, this time missing a vital spot kick against Peru in what turned out to be his final Scotland appearance.

TUESDAY 26TH AUGUST 1997

When Scotland international Darren Jackson pulled out of the Celtic squad for a European tie due to severe headaches on this day, he could scarcely have imagined what lay ahead. Jackson had hydrocephalus – water on the brain – and though his condition was not thought to be life-threatening, his football career was believed to be in serious jeopardy. Thankfully, a successful operation gave Jackson the chance to make a full recovery and he was back playing for Celtic within a few months. It turned out to be a spectacular season for him to enjoy as his club won both the league title and League Cup and Jackson also helped Scotland qualify for the World Cup in 1998. He played in two of the games in the finals in France, against Brazil and Norway.

TUESDAY 27TH AUGUST 1996

The SFA secured a continuing partnership with kit manufacturer Umbro when they signed a multi-million pound sponsorship deal. Umbro had produced Scotland kits for decades but after moving away from the usual design in recent seasons – the Euro 96 kit was based on a tartan pattern – it was announced that there would be a return to a more traditional look. The next Scotland home kit would be dark blue with a white collar and flashes on the sleeves.

TUESDAY 28TH AUGUST 1962

Duncan Shearer was born on this day in Fort William. He started his career with Inverness Clachnacuddin but moved south and after a few years at Chelsea, Huddersfield and Swindon, earned a big money move to Blackburn Rovers. Despite helping Rovers into the Premiership he failed to claim a regular starting spot and returned north to Aberdeen. It was at Pittodrie he finally forced himself into the international set-up and he scored twice in his first three games for Scotland. However, though he helped the team reach the finals of Euro 96, he did not feature in the tournament and finished his career with a total of seven Scotland caps.

SATURDAY 29TH AUGUST 1936

Bobby Ancell was transferred from St Mirren to Newcastle on this day, a move which would catapult him into the international side. Ancell had been a reliable performer for the Buddies and had helped them to a Scottish Cup Final and an immediate promotion after relegation in 1935. However, the full-back would not play a part in their next campaign as Newcastle swooped to secure his signature for a fee of £2,750. His impressive performances at St James' Park brought him recognition from Scotland and he earned his only caps when he played against Wales and Northern Ireland that year. After World War II interrupted his playing career, Ancell would go on to become a notable manager with several Scottish clubs.

MONDAY 29TH AUGUST 1994

Scotland's clubs in European competition had produced some dismal results in August 1994 but Craig Brown resisted the urge to make wholesale changes to the Scotland squad he named to face Finland. After taking charge for dead rubbers in the previous qualification campaign, this was his first truly competitive match and the manager was reluctant to take chances. Andy Walker – aged 29 and with just one cap – was the only newcomer and he was named alongside Eoin Jess, Pat Nevin and Duncan Shearer as the forwards. There was concern in the media about where the goals would come from but Shearer and midfielder John Collins would strike in each half to earn Scotland an important away win to start the campaign.

THURSDAY 30TH AUGUST 2001

Fifa stunned Europe's teams by giving them 24 hours' notice before making the play-off draw for the World Cup. Even though it was not yet known which countries would be competing for the final places in Japan and South Korea, the draw was done by pairing groups with each other. The runner-up in Scotland's group six would take on the equivalent country from group three which looked like being Denmark, Bulgaria or the Czech Republic.

WEDNESDAY 31ST AUGUST 1949

Scotland goalkeeper Stewart Kennedy was born in Stirling. After a slow start to his career, which saw him flit between the junior and senior game, he seemed to have made it in the mid-1970s when he earned a transfer to Rangers. He impressed enough at Ibrox to earn an international call-up and he looked set to establish himself as Scotland's number one until a disaster at Wembley. Kennedy was not the only culpable player but paid a heavy price as he was not picked again after a 5-1 defeat.

SATURDAY 31ST AUGUST 1968

Derek Whyte was born in Glasgow. Whyte played for Scotland over a period of several years but earned only 12 caps as while viewed as a reliable squad player, there usually seemed to be two or three others ahead of him for the starting berths. He had an excellent record for Scotland with the team not conceding a goal in the first seven games he played. In total he tasted defeat only once, winning six and drawing five of his games, but despite travelling to Italia 90, Euro 96 and France 98, he did not make an appearance at a major finals.

SATURDAY 31ST AUGUST 1996

The long road to France 98 started in Vienna with a match against Austria. Craig Brown's side turned in an efficient performance in claiming a very credible goalless draw, and with a little luck could even have secured all three points. In an experienced side, only four of the starting line-up had fewer than 20 caps to their name while six had over 30.

SCOTLAND
On This Day

SEPTEMBER

MONDAY 1st SEPTEMBER 1958

Matt Busby belatedly began his spell as manager after missing the 1958 World Cup to recuperate from the Munich air disaster. In charge for only two official games, he won the first in Wales before being held to a home draw by Northern Ireland. He would hand a debut to a young Huddersfield Town striker whom he would later sign for Manchester United – Denis Law.

SATURDAY 1st SEPTEMBER 2001

Scotland's World Cup hopes took a blow when they were held to a 0-0 draw at home by Croatia. While a draw against the best side in the group would not normally have been a disaster, the failure to beat Belgium at Hampden earlier in the campaign meant that points dropped at home had to be made up away. The side would travel to Brussels in midweek knowing defeat would all but end the chance of reaching the play-offs with the automatic qualifying place effectively out of reach already.

SATURDAY 2nd SEPTEMBER 2000

Though the World Cup dream had faded by 2001, in autumn 2000 Scotland made a sensational start to the qualifying campaign. Despite being badly outplayed in the opening game in Riga, they somehow managed to keep out an industrious Latvia side and Neil McCann slotted home a fortuitous winner in the last minute. With good results to follow in San Marino and Croatia there was no sign of the disappointment which was to come later.

SATURDAY 2nd SEPTEMBER 2006

A scheduling conflict meant that Scotland began their Euro 2008 qualifying campaign at Celtic Park rather than Hampden as Robbie Williams was playing a concert at the National Stadium! A crowd of over 50,000 went to the east, rather than south, side of Glasgow for the game against the Faroe Islands and were rewarded with a thrilling first-half performance which saw Scotland lead 5-0 at half-time. The goals, including two from the penalty spot, came from Darren Fletcher, James McFadden, Kenny Miller and a double from Kris Boyd. The second half was tame in comparison with only Garry O'Connor adding to the scoring.

WEDNESDAY 3RD SEPTEMBER 1958

An innovation was attempted in 1958 by having a training session on match day. Rangers trainer David Kinnear took a workout on the beach at Newcastle County Down before a game later in the evening against the Irish League. Whether the training session or low standard of the opposition was the greater factor in the 5-0 victory, earned in pouring rain, is up for debate!

WEDNESDAY 3RD SEPTEMBER 1975

Scotland still had a chance of qualifying for the European Championship finals in 1976 when they triumphed 1-0 against Denmark in Copenhagen. Joe Harper's goal capped a successful trip to Denmark as the under-23 side had also won the previous evening and the players had done enough to earn a night on the town. The scale of this little beano would only emerge the next day...

FRIDAY 3RD SEPTEMBER 2004

The weather tested Scotland again in 2004 but in Spain the elements came out on top. Scotland had stunned the hosts with a brilliant start to the game and earned an early lead through James McFadden's deflected free kick. Poor finishing and good goalkeeping kept Spain alive before they levelled from the penalty spot after the break. Only three minutes more could be played as a power cut caused by a lightning storm caused the game to be abandoned. It was only the second Scotland match of all time which did not reach its conclusion and, as in the previous instance against Austria in 1963, the game counted as a full international.

SATURDAY 3RD SEPTEMBER 2005

Proof that Scotland were getting back to their best after the disastrous Vogts years arrived when Italy were held to a draw at a raucous Hampden Park. Scotland, roared on by a Tartan Army which had seemingly made full use of two hours' extra drinking time afforded by the 5pm kick-off, more than matched the team which would go on to win the World Cup. The Italians needed a late deflection to claim a point but the damage from earlier in the campaign sadly could not be reversed.

THURSDAY 4TH SEPTEMBER 1975

The morning after the night before was not pleasant for Scotland as details began to emerge of what happened in Copenhagen. The riot police had been called to break up an early-hours scuffle in Bonnaparte's nightclub but the players, not heeding their warning, continued to celebrate at their hotel and eventually trashed a room. Joe Harper, Billy Bremner, Willie Young, Arthur Graham and Pat McCluskey were banned for life though Harper and Graham eventually played again. One international career which might have been saved by fate was that of Alan Rough – he took too long to leave the hotel and the taxi left without him.

SATURDAY 5TH SEPTEMBER 1931

Scottish football was thrown into mourning when Celtic goalkeeper John Thomson died in an Old Firm clash. Thomson, who had four caps for Scotland, was accidentally struck on the head by Sam English and despite immediate medical attention, died later in the evening. John Thomson was inducted into the Scottish Football Hall of Fame in 2008.

FRIDAY 5TH SEPTEMBER 1975

After the embarrassing revelations of the previous day, there was at least one small snippet from Copenhagen which could raise a smile. The *Glasgow Herald* reported that Willie Ormond had won a sweep on the result, organised by Danish journalists, and the manager quipped he had demanded possession football in the closing stages with Kenny Dalglish withdrawn to a deeper role!

SATURDAY 5TH SEPTEMBER 1998

Scotland's longest-ever run of games without a win reached nine when they were held to a 0-0 draw in Lithuania at the start of the Euro 2000 qualifying campaign. However, the spell of poor form can be put into some perspective as it included three games (Brazil, Norway, Morocco) at the World Cup finals and friendly matches before the tournament against future winners France, quarter-finalists Denmark and two further qualifiers in the shape of Colombia and the USA. The remaining match in the run was a 1-1 draw at home to Finland but with a little luck, Scotland could well have emerged victorious from several of the contests.

SATURDAY 6TH SEPTEMBER 1947

There has been only one player born in England who has gone on to captain the Scottish international team. Bruce Rioch, born on this day in Aldershot, was captain in ten of his 24 appearances in dark blue.

MONDAY 6TH SEPTEMBER 1971

Falkirk's Willie Cunningham had been offered the vacant post of Scotland manager but after some consideration turned it down. He explained his reasons at a Brockville press conference and even suggested the team be picked by committee with a panel of managers making the football decisions.

SATURDAY 6TH SEPTEMBER 2008

Scotland's first-ever trip to Macedonia was not a happy one as the side lost 1-0 under a blazing hot sun in Skopje. The Macedonians probably deserved the points over 90 minutes but they were blessed by good fortune when Scotland had two strong penalty claims denied. The Tartan Army also had problems as ground redevelopment severely limited the allocation of away tickets. While many countries allow Scotland fans into the home stands, the Macedonians refused this compromise meaning thousands of supporters failed to see the game despite many seats going unused.

WEDNESDAY 7TH SEPTEMBER 1977

Scottish goalkeepers were often a subject of comedy in years gone by but one who may feel harshly treated is Dave Stewart. The Leeds keeper earned his only cap in a 1-0 friendly defeat against East Germany and, although he saved a penalty, was never picked again.

SATURDAY 7TH SEPTEMBER 2002

Scotland almost reached an all-time low in this clash against the Faroe Islands. The part-time hosts ran riot in the first half and were two goals up in the opening 12 minutes. More could easily have had more before half-time. After the break Paul Lambert pulled one back and Barry Ferguson scored a late equaliser to salvage a draw but one player had had enough – Davie Weir made himself unavailable for selection as manager Berti Vogts singled out his performance for criticism.

WEDNESDAY 8TH SEPTEMBER 2004

Scotland have adjusted to taking on new countries on a regular basis and hosted Slovenia for the first time at the start of qualifying for the 2006 World Cup. Though the match finished in a disappointing 0-0 draw it was the proverbial game of two halves as Scotland controlled the first period and Slovenia the second. Neither side could make a breakthrough when on top but the guests were the much happier with a share of the points, as Scotland's campaign appeared to have stalled before it even started.

SATURDAY 8TH SEPTEMBER 2007

A disgraceful penalty decision threatened to damage Scotland's chances of reaching the finals of Euro 2008 but a late surge saw Lithuania defeated 3-1 at Hampden. Saulius Mikoliūnas' laughable dive somewhere in the same postcode as Darren Fletcher earned the equalising penalty but a goal from Stephen McManus and a superb strike from substitute James McFadden earned Scotland the points and set them up nicely for a crucial clash with France in midweek. Kris Boyd had headed a first-half opener from Darren Fletcher's quickly-taken free kick.

WEDNESDAY 9TH SEPTEMBER 1987

Rangers' prolific striker Ally McCoist needed time to adjust as he stepped up to international football and after six caps he was still waiting for his first goal. That all changed when he finally broke his duck against Hungary. Another goal came along immediately as he bagged a double in a 2-0 friendly win.

WEDNESDAY 9TH SEPTEMBER 1992

Scotland's World Cup campaign got off to the worst possible start in Berne when they lost 3-1 to Switzerland. Though Ally McCoist had cancelled out an early strike from the Swiss, the hosts were by far the better side and went on to win comfortably. The Scots misery was completed late on when Richard Gough was sent off for catching a long ball as it sailed over his head. It was the start of a sad end to Gough's long international career as he played only once more, in a 5-0 thrashing in Portugal, before quitting due to disagreements with manager Andy Roxburgh.

TUESDAY 10TH SEPTEMBER 1985

Delight at progressing to a play-off for the 1986 World Cup finals was quickly forgotten when Jock Stein collapsed towards the end of a game against Wales at Ninian Park, Cardiff. The Scots had needed a point to move into the play-off, where they would meet Australia. They were struggling against a strong Welsh side when Stein threw on Davie Cooper with around 20 minutes remaining. The fresh legs invigorated Scotland and when they were awarded a late penalty it was Cooper who converted the kick low to the left of Neville Southall. The celebrations of the Scotland players ended immediately after the full-time whistle, as they were informed of what had happened to the manager. Stein later died of a heart attack in the stadium's medical room. He will be remembered as a true colossus of the Scottish game, not only for guiding Scotland to the World Cup finals in 1982 but for his long list of achievements as a club manager with Dunfermline, Hibs and Celtic, the team he had led to the historic European Cup triumph of 1967.

WEDNESDAY 10TH SEPTEMBER 2003

Tempers frayed after Scotland lost to Germany by the odd goal in three at the Westfalenstadion, Dortmund. When manager Berti Vogts was being interviewed, Christian Dailly could be heard in the background, swearing loudly and calling the Germans cheats as he expressed his frustration at an apparent dive to earn the match-winning penalty.

WEDNESDAY 10TH SEPTEMBER 2008

At full-time in Reykjavik everyone was clear that Scotland had defeated Iceland 2-1 but who had scored the winning goal? James McFadden had lunged for a rebound after his own penalty had been saved but Barry Robson was also on hand as the ball was turned over the line. Newspaper reports and world governing body Fifa initially gave the credit to Robson but the SFA viewed television evidence and later appealed successfully to have the goal awarded to McFadden. Defender Kirk Broadfoot, whom manager George Burley had described before the game as having "limited ability", had scored the opener on his debut while Stephen McManus, who was playing on his birthday, was sent off late on for deliberate handball.

FRIDAY 11TH SEPTEMBER 1942

Rangers and Scotland legend John Greig was born in Edinburgh on this day. Greig was the sturdiest of defenders and holds the official appearance record for Rangers along with 44 Scotland caps. He made his international debut in 1964 and played in the famous Wembley triumph of 1967, but his talents were not shown to their best as he was a great player at the wrong time. He picked up the Cup Winners' Cup and 15 domestic honours, including five championships, but was up against the Celtic nine-in-a-row team of the 1960s and 70s for a substantial part of his career. Similarly with Scotland, the side, despite boasting several top players, did not reach any major finals when he was at his peak and although capped for the last time in 1975, his penultimate appearance in dark blue had been in 1971. Scoring was not his forte and Greig bagged only three Scotland goals but one of these was a famous last-minute winner against Italy at Hampden.

WEDNESDAY 11TH SEPTEMBER 1991

In a tight qualifying group featuring Switzerland, Romania and Bulgaria (and whipping boys San Marino), Scotland took an important step towards the finals of Euro 92 with a dramatic comeback in Berne. The Swiss were looking good for the points when two goals up but Gordon Durie pulled one back before Ally McCoist's late equaliser, with only seven minutes remaining, kept Scotland's hopes alive.

WEDNESDAY 12TH SEPTEMBER 2007

What many believe to be Scotland's finest-ever performance and result came in Paris against World Cup finalists France as they looked to qualify for the 2008 European Championships. Everyone remembers James McFadden's wonder goal which won the points but along with a reliable goalkeeper and solid defence, Scotland excelled at keeping the ball when in possession. If the win at home to France the previous year had been fortunate – the guests hit the post and had a goal disallowed for a marginal offside decision – this victory was anything but lucky. Scotland restricted France to no more than a few clear chances as the points took them to the top of the group and within touching distance of glory.

JAMES MCFADDEN'S STUNNING GOAL IN PARIS EARNED SCOTLAND A FAMOUS VICTORY OVER FRANCE.

MONDAY 13TH SEPTEMBER 1993

After 61 games in charge of the national team, manager Andy Roxburgh resigned. Roxburgh left because the side had failed to reach the World Cup finals in America but the results in the campaign, in what was admittedly a brutally tough group, had been bitterly disappointing. Roxburgh had enjoyed a modest playing career before moving into coaching with the SFA rather than a club side, effectively preparing for the manager's job over a number of years. He had led the under-18 side to Scotland's only official title in the 1982 European Championships but critics – pointing to his fall-outs with Richard Gough – claimed he was unable to deal with top players. However, on the whole his time was considered a success as he had not only led Scotland to one World Cup finals in 1990 but also the finals of the European Championship, in 1992, for the first time.

WEDNESDAY 14TH SEPTEMBER 1988

Scotland made the perfect start to qualifying for Italia 90 by winning 2-1 against Norway in Oslo. The side had missed out on the European Championships held earlier in the year in West Germany but showed an early determination not to miss out on the next finals. A fine strike from Paul McStay, and a typical poacher's effort from Mo Johnston, claimed the points.

FRIDAY 15TH SEPTEMBER 2006

Fans queued overnight to be first in line at Hampden Park when tickets for the forthcoming France game went on sale. Demand was sky high after Scotland had made a winning start to the group with victories over the Faroe Islands and Lithuania, and those who received tickets for the France game would not be disappointed.

THURSDAY 16TH SEPTEMBER 2004

Despite its history of massive attendances, Hampden Park is no longer the biggest ground in Scotland. That honour now falls to the Murrayfield rugby stadium in Edinburgh but a few football matches have now taken place there as well. The first goal ever scored at Murrayfield was in 2004 as Scotland defender Andy Webster headed Hearts in front against Braga in an eventual 3-1 win.

SATURDAY 17TH SEPTEMBER 1938

Scotland's great striker Hughie Gallacher was approaching the end of his career but proved he had not lost his scoring touch for Gateshead. On this day he scored five for his team against Rotherham United to achieve the feat for the fifth time. He had previously scored five goals in a game for Airdrie, the Scottish League, Scotland and Derby County but ironically had failed to do so for Newcastle, the club with whom he is most commonly associated.

MONDAY 18TH SEPTEMBER 1978

The future of Hampden Park was still looking bleak late in the 1970s as Queen's Park were running out of money to pay for necessary upgrades. The club, and the stadium as a result, was bailed out on this day when Queen's were given £60,000 to help meet safety standards laid down by Strathclyde Regional Council. It was believed that the money had been given by the SFA, from cash they had intended to use on Hampden in the future, though none of the SFA, Queen's Park or the Council would confirm the source. There were ambitious plans for Hampden around this time with hopes of a new North Stand, substantial renovation to the South Stand and fully covered terracing, but problems raising the capital required for such a project meant they never became a reality. Instead Hampden was patched up time and time again to meet safety requirements with the capacity tumbling to less than 70,000. A proper redevelopment of the ground was undertaken only when enforced by the Taylor Report following the 1989 Hillsborough tragedy and by that point several people suggested that there was no real need for a national stadium as Scotland games could be taken round the country.

SATURDAY 19TH SEPTEMBER 1931

Scotland made a winning start to the 1932 British Home Championship when they defeated Northern Ireland 3-1 at Ibrox. Motherwell's George Stevenson opened the scoring but the Irish proved stubborn opponents and promptly equalised. Jimmy McGrory of Celtic restored the lead before local hero Bob McPhail secured the points with a third goal late on. Scotland defeated Wales away in their next championship game but a loss at Wembley to England cost them their chance of the title.

TUESDAY 20th SEPTEMBER 1983

Andy Beattie, Scotland's first manager, died on this day aged 70. World War II greatly disrupted his playing career but he became an astute manager and was involved with several clubs in England. His efforts at managing the national team cannot be compared fairly with his modern successors as the circumstances he worked under are almost unimaginable now. Not only was he part-time, the SFA restricted his authority and he was infuriated when allowed to take only 13 players to the 1954 World Cup finals rather than the full complement allowed by Fifa. He resigned during that tournament and although he returned for a brief second spell a few years later, Andy Beattie will be remembered as a pioneering manager who was not given the resources to make a fair fist of his task.

SUNDAY 21st SEPTEMBER 1969

Scotland's 1-1 friendly draw with the Republic of Ireland was probably more important for Colin Stein than anyone else. He found the net for the sixth time in a row in games played for his country, equalling Robert Hamilton's record at the turn of the century.

WEDNESDAY 21st SEPTEMBER 1977

Scotland faced a crunch game with Czechoslovakia as they looked to increase their chances of progression to the World Cup finals. Goals from Joe Jordan, Asa Hartford and Kenny Dalglish made the game safe against a Czech side who, despite being European champions, seemed intimidated by the passionate Hampden atmosphere. The guests did score a late consolation but all eyes had already turned to the final game, against Wales in a few weeks, which would decide Scotland's fate.

MONDAY 22nd SEPTEMBER 1980

The English FA council met in London and decided that no tickets would be sent north for the visit of Scotland to Wembley the following May. This was widely expected following trouble at the previous two meetings. FA secretary Ted Croker said this would be the "last chance" for the fixture but the Scottish fans started to make preparations for their annual invasion regardless and eventually made up a substantial part of the 90,000 crowd.

MONDAY 23RD SEPTEMBER 1946

Jim McCalliog was born on this day in Glasgow in 1946 and would later write his name into the Scottish football history books with a goal on his international debut. McCalliog had already caught the eye at Chelsea but became Britain's most expensive teenager when transferred to Sheffield Wednesday. He tasted FA Cup Final defeat with the Owls but his return to Wembley would be a spectacular success. His international debut came in the famous 1967 win over England and it was McCalliog who scored the third, and winning, goal in the contest. Unfortunately, his international career did not take off as he would have hoped and although he played another four games for Scotland he failed to find the net again for his country. The other highlight of his career also came at Wembley when he helped Southampton win the FA Cup Final 1-0 against Manchester United in 1976.

MONDAY 24TH SEPTEMBER 1958

Though Paul Lambert is well known for his time at Borussia Dortmund, he was not the first Scottish international midfielder to take the Bundesliga by storm. Murdo MacLeod, born on this day, enjoyed a successful three-year spell with the Ruhr giants from 1987 to 1990. MacLeod's career had begun at Dumbarton but he came to prominence with Celtic as a tough midfielder who was capable of scoring spectacular goals from distance with thunderbolt shots. After years of success in Glasgow, Murdo decided to try his luck abroad and fared well with his new team, winning the German Cup with a 4-1 thrashing of Werder Bremen in 1989. He established himself in the Scotland side during this time and collected 20 caps in total, the highlight of which was probably the 1990 World Cup win over Sweden in Genoa. Murdo moved back to Scotland with Hibs, where he won the League Cup. Later in life – and following spells as manager of Dumbarton and Partick Thistle and as assistant manager to Wim Jansen at Celtic – he began working in the media. September 24th is one of the most common dates of birth for post-war Scottish internationals. Along with Murdo MacLeod, it is also the birthday of John O'Hare (1946), Ally McCoist (1962), Gary McSwegan (1970) and Craig Burley (1971). The quintet has a combined total of 142 caps and 29 goals for Scotland.

MONDAY 25TH SEPTEMBER 1961

The Scotland selection committee held an afternoon meeting on this day to determine the team which would face Czechoslovakia in the World Cup qualifiers. Having already lost away to the Czechs, a victory seemed required here to force a play-off as the Eastern Europeans were expected to defeat the Republic of Ireland in their remaining games. Scotland trailed twice but two goals by Denis Law secured a 3-2 victory and kept alive hopes of reaching the finals in Chile.

WEDNESDAY 26TH SEPTEMBER 1973

Scotland's Hampden clash with Czechoslovakia, 12 years to the day of a previous meeting, was not actually a do or die game, as the sides would meet again in Bratislava later in the year. However, it was generally accepted that a result would not be forthcoming against such a strong side behind the Iron Curtain so Scotland's chance of reaching the World Cup finals in West Germany hinged on a home win here. A stirring comeback from a goal down was started by Jim Holton's towering header and when Joe Jordan scored a late header of his own, Scotland could look out their passports for their first finals appearance in 16 years.

TUESDAY 26TH SEPTEMBER 1978

An era ended when Ally MacLeod resigned his post with Scotland. The side had played only one game since returning from the disastrous World Cup campaign in Argentina but the fact that it was lost made little difference – the only questions surrounding MacLeod's departure were if he'd jump before he was pushed. The SFA later confirmed that his position was untenable and he would have been sacked but they had felt unable to do so immediately after the side returned to Scotland. Instead, MacLeod was given a respectable amount of time – a generous touch which one suspects would not happen today. MacLeod did well in charge of Ayr United but eventually ended his managerial career at Queen of the South. A last smile was raised when an injury crisis left the reserves short so Ally, into his 60s, donned his boots and played one last time. He even scored a penalty kick before receiving a standing ovation from the few fans in attendance as he walked into retirement.

WEDNESDAY 27TH SEPTEMBER 1989

Tommy Hutchison was once the oldest player to take part in a European tie, aged 42, but his Swansea City side exited the Cup Winners' Cup on this day in 1989 as they went out 6-5 on aggregate to Panathinaikos. They were held to a 3-3 draw at home a couple of weeks after losing 3-2 in Athens but for Hutchison it was just one more step in an extraordinary career. He had started with Alloa before moving to Blackpool and then Coventry City, where he won 17 Scottish caps. He helped the side reach the World Cup finals in 1974 and played in West Germany against both Zaire and Yugoslavia. He went to Swansea via Manchester City, for whom he scored – at both ends – in the 1981 FA Cup Final.

WEDNESDAY 27TH SEPTEMBER 1995

Only one player has cost a non-Old Firm club in Scotland a seven-figure transfer fee and that is the twice-capped Paul Bernard. Though born in Edinburgh, he took his first steps in league football with Oldham Athletic and featured in the last few games of their promotion season in 1991. He needed time to win a regular place in their top-flight side but soon established himself as a hardworking midfielder. He would be badly injured on international duty with the Scotland under-21 side and unfortunately that would become a regular problem. He had made his Scotland debut as he played both games against Japan and Ecuador in the 1995 Kirin Cup when Aberdeen splashed out £1m on this day to secure his signature. Injury made it hard for him to make an impact and though he reached three finals with the club, winning the League Cup, he was eventually released on a free transfer.

WEDNESDAY 28TH SEPTEMBER 1966

Hearts sacked manager Tommy Walker on this day. He had played with the Tynecastle club and was arguably the finest Scottish inside-forward of his day, gaining 21 caps and scoring nine goals. Under his management they won the league twice and were runners-up five times. They also won the Scottish Cup in 1956 and the League Cup in 1955, 1960 and 1963 before the board decided a change was needed.

FRIDAY 29TH SEPTEMBER 1939

Jim Baxter was born in Hill o' Beath on September 29th, 1939 just a few weeks after the start of World War II. His football career started with a local club in Fife before he made his first step up to Raith Rovers, where he continued to impress. Rangers were next to call and it is with the Glasgow team and Scotland he is most often associated. His superb close control and range of passing allowed him to dominate virtually any midfield but even in his best days at Ibrox his liking for alcohol and the high life were becoming noted. He had already starred in one Wembley victory for Scotland in 1963 before he was sold to Sunderland by Rangers and his powers seemed to be in decline. There was still magic left though and he inspired Scotland to a 3-2 victory over the world champions at Wembley in 1967 when his keepie-uppie became an iconic image of a Gallus Scot player taunting the defeated English.

SATURDAY 30TH SEPTEMBER 1944

Jimmy Johnstone, one of Viewpark's finest sons, was born on this day. Johnstone was a mercurial talent who shone for the great Celtic side of the 1960s and 70s and was part of the European Cup-winning team in 1967. He was not included in the side which defeated England at Wembley a few weeks after that game, and also experienced disappointment in 1974 when although taken to the World Cup, he was not selected to play. Instead, Johnstone's greatest moments usually came in the hoops of Celtic. Illness claimed his life at the age of 61 in 2006.

FRIDAY 30TH SEPTEMBER 1966

John Prentice was a stop-gap manager who had been appointed to lead the team through a number of friendly matches and the final game in the British Home Championship of 1966. The part-time nature of the job made it difficult to make a good impression and Prentice eventually left at the end of September after six months in charge. However, the next incumbent, Malcolm McDonald, would spend even less time in the job, so the problems the SFA had in finding a manager would not be resolved immediately!

SCOTLAND
On This Day

OCTOBER

SATURDAY 1st OCTOBER 1949

Henry Morris of East Fife must have wondered just what he did wrong not to earn a second Scotland cap. His first performance, in Scotland's 8-2 thrashing of Northern Ireland, was certainly a startling introduction to international football as he bagged a hat-trick, outscoring famous names such as Billy Steel and Laurie Reilly, who managed only one each. Nonetheless, if Morris was expecting a second call-up he was to be disappointed and this remained the only appearance for his country. This match was also Scotland's first-ever World Cup contest as the British Home Championship of 1949/50 was used by Fifa to determine who would travel to Brazil the next summer.

SATURDAY 2nd OCTOBER 1965

Despite a double from Alan Gilzean, Scotland lost 3-2 to Northern Ireland in the opening game of the 1966 British Home Championship. He had put the guests in front in Belfast and equalised with eight minutes remaining, but this was not enough to force a draw for Scotland as they conceded a last-gasp winner.

SATURDAY 3rd OCTOBER 1953

After declining to take the place they had earned at the 1950 World Cup, Scotland made a good start to the qualifying campaign for the 1954 tournament with a 3-1 win against Northern Ireland in Belfast. However, this would turn out to be Scotland's only victory in the whole competition. A draw and a defeat in the remaining British Home Championship games secured qualification to Switzerland where Scotland lost both matches against Austria and Uruguay.

FRIDAY 3rd OCTOBER 1958

Jackie Henderson was a latecomer to football and only began playing the game as a teenager but still went on to represent Scotland. On this day in 1958 Arsenal paid £20,000 to Wolves for his services and the attacker – who could play up front or on either wing – did well for the side at a time when the club was generally struggling. The majority of his seven Scottish caps had arrived when still with his first club, Portsmouth, but his form at Highbury was good enough to earn him a brief recall.

WEDNESDAY 4TH OCTOBER 1978

Jock Stein was appointed manager of Scotland as he ended a difficult period in charge of Leeds United after only 45 days. The manager was leading his country for the second time but after his challenging part-time role of the 1960s, things would be very different on this occasion. He took the job on a full-time basis and had a much bigger say over team matters than previously. Under his leadership the side would fail to progress from the group stage of the 1982 World Cup finals – only on goal difference – and Scotland were on course to reach the finals in Mexico in 1986 when he died of a heart attack in 1985.

MONDAY 4TH OCTOBER 1993

Jim Holton died suddenly on this day, aged 42. The tall defender played 15 times for Scotland and had a crucial role in guiding Scotland to the World Cup in 1974. Czechoslovakia had stunned Hampden Park with the opening goal in a vital qualifier when Jim Holton powered home a header from a corner to equalise. Joe Jordan scored the winner and Holton, along with the rest of the squad, was off to West Germany. He played in all three games at the finals but earned only one more cap as the two leg breaks he suffered at Manchester United signalled the end of his best years.

SATURDAY 5TH OCTOBER 1996

Latvia hosted Scotland for the first time in this World Cup qualifier for France 98. Scotland toiled but eventually won 2-0 thanks to two fine goals in the second half. A well worked free-kick routine allowed John Collins to open the scoring before Darren Jackson enjoyed some good fortune on the evening of his 13th cap, notching his first international goal to seal victory.

TUESDAY 5TH OCTOBER 1999

Scotland took a decisive step towards the play-offs for Euro 2000 with a 1-0 win at home to Bosnia. Having already defeated the Balkan side away, the path was now relatively straightforward for Craig Brown's men to finish second behind runaway leaders the Czech Republic.

SATURDAY 6TH OCTOBER 2001

Scotland's World Cup dreams ended despite defeating Latvia 2-1 at Hampden. The side had been placed in a near impossible position after losing the previous game in Belgium and had to win this contest by a huge margin to have any chance of progression. Goals from Dougie Freedman, his only strike for Scotland, and Davie Weir secured the victory on the day but were not nearly enough. In the dressing room manager Craig Brown informed the players of his intention to resign immediately after the game.

SATURDAY 7TH OCTOBER 2000

Patience was the name of the game as Scotland eventually triumphed 2-0 away to San Marino on this day in 2000. The squad must have been dreading the thought of the newspaper headlines the next day as the clock ticked past the hour mark with the tie still goalless, but eventually the breakthrough came with just 19 minutes remaining. Matt Elliott headed the opener and Don Hutchison's chip ensured Scotland would avoid embarrassment.

SATURDAY 7TH OCTOBER 2006

Gary Caldwell became a hero as he scored the only goal of the game as Scotland defeated France 1-0 at Hampden. The French team may not have contained Zinedine Zidane but they were still one of the best in the world and hot favourites for this match. Scotland lived on their nerves in the first half as France struck the post and had a couple of goals disallowed for offside. But, Caldwell converted Hartley's corner after the break sparking bedlam among the home support. Scotland held on to make it three wins out of three at the start of the Euro 2008 qualifying campaign.

WEDNESDAY 7TH OCTOBER 2009

Diadora's financial troubles meant that the SFA were suddenly left without a kit supplier to the national team. After some months of uncertainty, it was eventually confirmed that leading brand Adidas would supply the new jerseys along with the usual assortment of training and leisure wear. Some heavier members of the Tartan Army expressed relief that another manufacturer with a tendency to produce skin-tight strips had not been chosen instead!

SATURDAY 8TH OCTOBER 1988

Ian Durrant was one of the brightest talents in Scottish football when he suffered a horrific injury at Pittodrie. He eventually recovered after a substantial period out of the game but despite earning 20 caps in total his magnificent potential arguably remained unfulfilled.

SATURDAY 8TH OCTOBER 2005

It was confirmed another World Cup would be taking place without Scotland as Belarus won 1-0 at Hampden to end the dream for another four years. Walter Smith had picked up the pieces after Berti Vogts' reign had threatened to end the qualifying campaign almost before it had begun, but fell just short of reaching the finals. A sensational win in Oslo had kept hope alive going into this game but the Scots looked nervous and fell behind to an early goal. Despite a spell of half-hearted pressure there would be no equaliser, never mind a winner, and Scotland exited the tournament with a whimper rather than a bang.

WEDNESDAY 9TH OCTOBER 1996

When the Tartan Army sang 'There's only one team in Tallinn' in 1996 they were not quite factually correct. There were two teams in Tallinn but the problem was that one remained at a hotel to prepare for the game while the other was on the pitch taking the kick-off! Scotland had successfully appealed to have the game brought forward because of poor floodlighting but the Estonians refused to play ball and insisted the match go ahead as scheduled in the evening. Despite the rules saying Scotland should be awarded a 3-0 victory, Uefa eventually ordered the match be replayed in Monaco.

SATURDAY 9TH OCTOBER 2004

After drawing 0-0 at home to Slovenia in the opening game of the World Cup 2006 qualifying group, Scotland desperately needed to defeat Norway. Instead they lost 1-0 to a second-half penalty after James McFadden had been sent off for deliberately handling on the line. Though this was a poor performance, things may have been different had Richard Hughes been awarded a goal when he appeared to scramble the ball over the line from a first-half corner.

SATURDAY 10TH OCTOBER 1998

Jim Leighton became the oldest player to feature for Scotland at 40 years, two months and 16 days of age when he played in goal against Estonia. Unfortunately, this was not his best game as he conceded twice in a 3-2 success. The match was also notable for being Ally McCoist's last appearance for Scotland.

WEDNESDAY 11TH OCTOBER 1989

Scotland missed the chance to secure qualification for Italia 90 when they were hammered 3-0 in Paris. Steve Nicol had particular reason to forget the game as he became the first Scot to score own goals in consecutive matches having put through his own net in the loss to Yugoslavia.

SATURDAY 11TH OCTOBER 1998

Scotland's 1,100th goal was scored by Gordon Durie against Latvia but more significant was the 2-0 win which effectively secured passage to France 98. Scotland did not win the qualifying group but were the best runner-up and thus missed out on the need for a two-game play-off to reach the finals.

WEDNESDAY 11TH OCTOBER 2006

Steven Pressley became the first Scottish player to play two matches on his birthday when the team lost 2-0 to Ukraine. His other birthday appearance was similarly unfortunate as that brought a 1-0 loss to Lithuania in Kaunas in 2003. At least on that occasion Pressley lasted the full game as in Kiev he was shown a late red card for a professional foul.

SATURDAY 11TH OCTOBER 2008

While most players will remember their international debuts with fondness, Chris Iwelumo will look back on this match against Norway with a hint of regret. He inexplicably missed an open goal from six yards when Scotland looked certain to take the lead and as no breakthrough was made, the points were shared in a goalless draw. That miss apart, Iwelumo actually played well during his time on the pitch but his introduction as a substitute rather than Kris Boyd was a highly controversial decision by manager Burley.

WEDNESDAY 12TH OCTOBER 1977

"Argentina, here we come!" was the cry by commentator Arthur Montford when Kenny Dalglish's sensational header secured a 2-0 win over Wales at Anfield. The victory meant Scotland topped their qualifying group ahead of Wales and Czechoslovakia but had earned the points in controversial circumstances. They had been awarded a penalty after Joe Jordan, rather than Welsh defender Dave Jones, appeared to handle in the box. The Scot later denied the offence but the 'hand of Jord', as well as the 1986 hand of God, still raises a smile in Scotland and causes resentment in Wales. The Welsh FA had chosen to play the game at Anfield to maximise revenue as they were unable to play the match at their usual ground in Cardiff. Though Liverpool is close to the Welsh border, a huge travelling army from Scotland more than cancelled out any home advantage the hosts hoped to gain.

WEDNESDAY 12TH OCTOBER 1994

Scotland faced the Faroe Islands for the first time when they came to Hampden in 1994. They had already caused a sensation by defeating Austria in 1990 but the Scots were alert and strolled to a comfortable 5-1 win. The Islanders and their small group of fans still celebrated lustily when they notched a late consolation with a well worked goal.

MONDAY 12TH OCTOBER 1998

Jim Leighton ended his Scotland career, which spanned almost 16 years, after criticism of his last performance against Estonia. Manager Craig Brown later revealed: "I got a call from Jim telling me what he intended to do. I tried to dissuade him but he said he just wanted to bow out quietly."

SUNDAY 12TH OCTOBER 2008

Quitting was also in vogue ten years later when Kris Boyd announced he no longer wished to be considered for selection by manager George Burley. Boyd had been left on the bench as debutant Chris Iwelumo was thrown on against Norway the day before, but he had rarely featured under Burley and in quitting cited he was following the manager's advice to focus on becoming a regular for his club Rangers.

TUESDAY 13TH OCTOBER 1970

There was concern for Scotland as Leeds United revealed they were considering moving one of their games in April forward to November, causing a clash with the World Cup qualifying tie in Austria. Leeds were anxious to avoid a repeat of their hectic end-of-season schedule at the end of the previous campaign, but if successful their plan would mean Eddie Gray and Billy Bremner would be unavailable for the Scottish match.

WEDNESDAY 14TH OCTOBER 1936

Germany made history by becoming the first country to fly to Glasgow for an international game. A triple engine Junkers aircraft brought the squad to Renfrew in preparation for their match at Ibrox where, upon lining up on the pitch, they gave the Nazi salute customary of the time. Scotland were not distracted by the crude political gesture and two second-half goals from Jimmy Delaney brought a 2-0 win against the guests.

SATURDAY 14TH OCTOBER 1944

Scotland introduced an innovation to their kits for a wartime international with England in 1944. Numbers were worn on the shirts for the first time but there were few other positives to remember from a game Scotland lost 6-2. The visitors had led at half-time but a Tommy Lawton hat-trick inspired the hosts to a comfortable victory.

WEDNESDAY 14TH OCTOBER 1992

After losing their opening World Cup qualifier in Switzerland, Scotland were anxious to get back on track with the first of two home games against Portugal and Italy. The side were unable to use Hampden Park due to building works so Ibrox was the venue. The ground was only just half full as less than 23,000 turned up. Scotland's side contained talented creative players like John Collins, Paul McStay and Gary McAllister but no-one was able to spark the breakthrough which was needed to win this game. That would be Scotland's problem throughout the group as Italy and Switzerland would also leave Glasgow and Aberdeen respectively with draws, giving the side a very difficult task in Lisbon and Rome to make up the points needed to qualify.

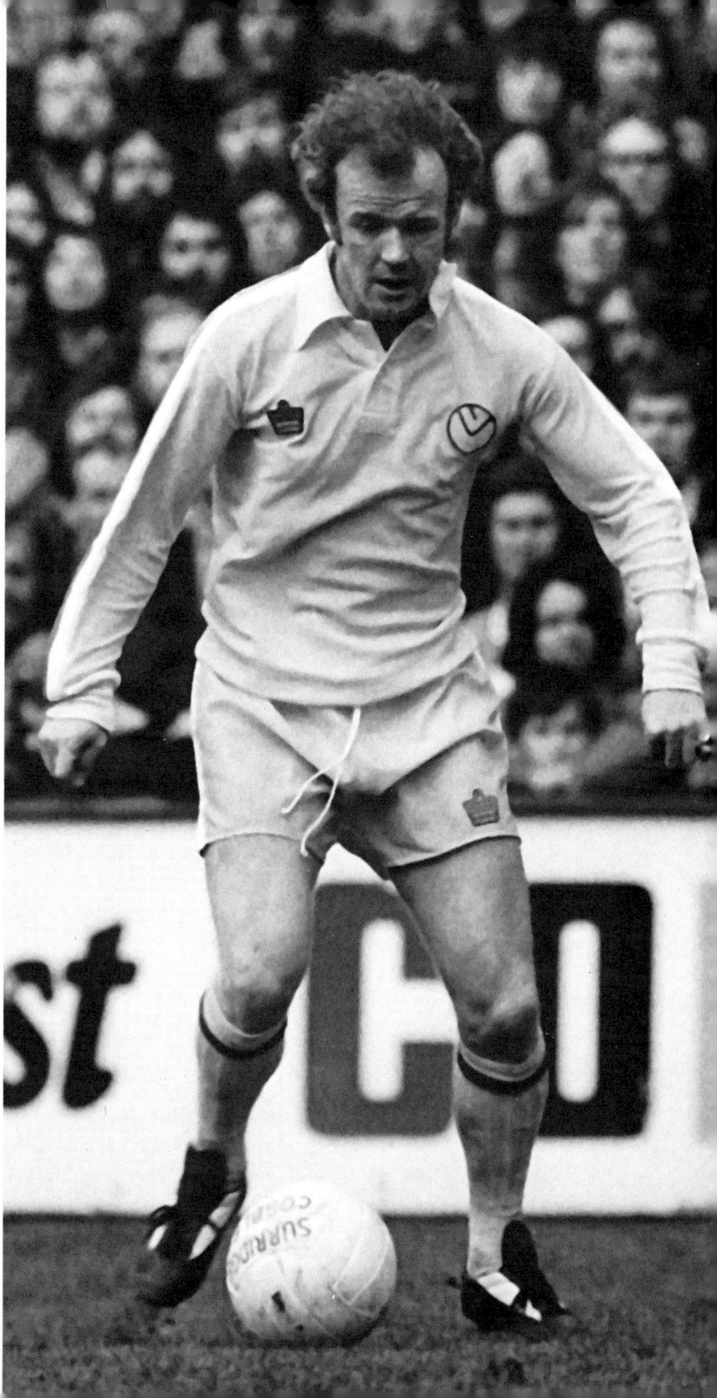

SCOTLAND CAPTAIN BILLY BREMNER IN ACTION FOR LEEDS UNITED.

TUESDAY 15TH OCTOBER 1985

Following the death of Jock Stein, assistant manager Alex Ferguson took charge of the national team. Ferguson would remain as boss of Aberdeen while, assisted by Jim McLean of Dundee United, having the short-term goal of guiding the side through a two-legged play-off with Australia to reach the 1986 World Cup finals.

WEDNESDAY 16TH OCTOBER 1991

Scotland's Euro 92 hopes were left hanging by a thread when they went down 1-0 to a late penalty in Bucharest against Romania. Even a draw would have been enough to seal qualification – assuming that group whipping boys San Marino were beaten at Hampden in the final game – but it was not to be. Instead Romania became most likely to top the group but had to win both of their remaining games at home to Switzerland, and away to Bulgaria, and hope to pip Scotland on goal difference.

WEDNESDAY 17TH OCTOBER 1984

Iceland met Scotland for the first-ever time when they lost 3-0 in Glasgow. Paul McStay dominated the midfield in this clash and scored one of the best goals seen at Hampden with a tremendous drive high into the postage stamp corner from more than 30 yards.

WEDNESDAY 17TH OCTOBER 1990

Scotland struck an early blow in the Euro 92 qualifying campaign when they defeated Switzerland 2-1 at Hampden Park thanks to a super goal by Gary McAllister. Ally McCoist missed an early penalty but when the Scots were awarded a second spot kick John Robertson confidently smashed it home. It was his second international goal in as many games but his next 14 caps would bring only one more strike.

WEDNESDAY 17TH OCTOBER 2007

After defeating Ukraine at Hampden in the first match after the high of success in Paris, the Scotland Euro 2008 bandwagon rolled into Tbilisi and the wheels came off completely. A side rearranged due to several injuries never looked comfortable and goals in each half gave the hosts a deserved win.

SATURDAY 18TH OCTOBER 1958

Scotland recorded a crushing win over an impressive Wales side which had been knocked out of the World Cup earlier in the summer by eventual winners Brazil. The game is notable for Denis Law making his full international debut, and scoring, before he had turned 19 years old. Law's goal was sandwiched between strikes from Graham Leggat and Bobby Collins and would be the first of 30, an all-time record, he would score for Scotland.

WEDNESDAY 18TH OCTOBER 1972

Scotland had high hopes of gaining a World Cup win in Denmark when they started the qualifying group for the 1974 World Cup and though the team duly delivered, the nature of the victory raised eyebrows. The Danes had come out on top the last time they met in their capital but on this occasion they were simply blown away by a brilliant performance. Jimmy Bone, Lou Macari, Joe Harper and Willie Morgan claimed the goals as the Scots were simply wonderful in Copenhagen and convincingly won 4-1.

MONDAY 19TH OCTOBER 1981

Johnny Doyle, who had been capped once against Romania in 1975, was electrocuted in a domestic accident on this day. The lively winger started at Ayr United before being snapped up by Celtic and he had established himself as a favourite at Parkhead before his place came under threat from the emergence of another Scotland winger, Davie Provan.

WEDNESDAY 19TH OCTOBER 1988

The honour of scoring Scotland's 1,000th goal fell to Maurice Johnston as he secured a 1-1 draw against Yugoslavia in a World Cup qualifier. Scotland had built on a good opening away win in Oslo by drawing at home with the Yugoslavs who would be the dominant force in the group.

SATURDAY 20TH OCTOBER 1962

Scotland's scorers in the 3-2 win over Wales in 1962 reads like an entry list to the hall of fame – Eric Caldow grabbed the first, Scotland's 700th, before Denis Law and Willie Henderson also chipped in.

WEDNESDAY 21st OCTOBER 1964

With the next World Cup finals being held over the border in England, there was big pressure to qualify. Things started brightly in the qualifying group as Finland were defeated 3-1 in Glasgow with goals from Denis Law, Stevie Chalmers and Davie Gibson but Poland and Italy would prove much sterner opposition...

THURSDAY 22nd OCTOBER 1964

Future Scotland player and manager Craig Levein was born in Dunfermline on this day. He would start his professional career at Cowdenbeath before moving to Hearts, where he impressed enough to earn the first of 16 Scotland caps in the 1990 friendly win against world champions Argentina. He did well enough to retain his place in the build-up games to Italia 90 but at the finals he played in only one of the three matches, though at least he tasted victory and had a superb personal performance against Sweden. A fierce competitor, he was once involved in a fight with a teammate in a pre-season friendly at Raith Rovers! Knee trouble caused him to retire prematurely from playing and after serving his managerial apprenticeship at his first club, Cowdenbeath, he went on to achieve success at Hearts and Dundee United either side of a problematic spell at Leicester City. Notably, he was responsible for revolutionising the way youth football is coached at Tannadice and that would have impressed the SFA as they appointed him Scotland manager with responsibility for leading the team out of the international wilderness and to the finals of Euro 2012. His first match proved a success as a battling performance earned a 1-0 friendly victory against qualifying group rivals the Czech Republic.

WEDNESDAY 22nd OCTOBER 1969

Scotland put up a good fight in Hamburg's Volksparkstadion but West Germany eventually proved too strong and they won 3-2 in this World Cup qualifier. Despite a good start in the group, this loss to the favourites ended Scotland's chances of going to Mexico in 1970 and they went on to lose the final qualifying game to Austria in Vienna as well. Jimmy Johnstone and Alan Gilzean grabbed the goals with Tommy Gemmell being sent off for a retaliatory kick at Helmut Haller late in the match.

TUESDAY 23RD OCTOBER 1973

Christian Dailly, one of Scotland's most committed players in modern times, was born in Dundee on this day. The flexible player broke into the Dundee United team as a teenager and initially started out as a striker. His potential quickly earned international recognition with the under-21s with whom he played for several years before finishing with a world record 34 appearances. As his career progressed he dropped to deeper positions and eventually settled as a commanding defender, or defensive midfielder, although he also deputised at times on either side of the field as a full-back. Derby County, Blackburn Rovers, West Ham United and Rangers were notable stops on his path but he also accumulated 67 caps for Scotland, scoring six goals. He played in all three games at the 1998 World Cup finals, and in both victories over France in the Euro 2008 qualifying group, but perhaps his finest 90 minutes was a magnificent display in the 1-0 Euro 2004 play-off victory over Holland at Hampden. He tussled superbly with the cream of the Dutch side but a booking ruled him out of the second leg through suspension. Scotland collapsed to lose 6-0 in Amsterdam and the Christian Dailly-shaped gap in the middle of the park was all too apparent.

SATURDAY 24TH OCTOBER 1908

Great Britain won the football gold medal at the London Olympics of 1908 but even then Scotland had nothing to do with it as the team was the English amateur side rather than a mixture from the Home Nations. Around 100 years later the SFA had to fight bitterly to ensure Scotland's identity as a separate football nation was not threatened by the emergence of a new Team GB for the London Olympics of 2012. A compromise was reached as it was agreed only English players would be considered for selection.

WEDNESDAY 24TH OCTOBER 2007

The much maligned Fifa World Rankings were being taken more seriously by the Tartan Army – if only a little – in October 2007 when Scotland reached their highest-ever position of 13th. Home and away wins over France, and an impressive triumph against Ukraine in the latest qualifying group, helped boost the ranking.

WEDNESDAY 25TH OCTOBER 1944

Former Scottish international Donald Ford was born in Linlithgow on this day. Though he had a formidable scoring record for Hearts, and went to the World Cup finals in 1974, he could not make a place his own in the strong Scottish side of the day and finished his career with three caps. His debut came in the dead rubber against Czechoslovakia in 1973 but although he made the trip to West Germany he had to settle for watching from the sidelines. He scored several hat-tricks for Hearts including one which consisted solely of penalty kicks in a victory over Morton. After football he developed his skills in photography and opened the Donald Ford Gallery.

WEDNESDAY 25TH OCTOBER 1978

Scotland had lost the opening game of the qualification group to the 1980 European Championships but bounced back with a 3-2 win at home to Norway thanks to goals from Kenny Dalglish (2) and Archie Gemmill. The match was notable for the line-up which consisted entirely of players from English clubs: Jim Stewart (Middlesbrough), Willie Donachie (Manchester City), Frank Gray (Leeds United), Graeme Souness (Liverpool), Gordon McQueen (Manchester United), Martin Buchan (Manchester United), Kenny Dalglish (Liverpool), Archie Gemmill (Nottingham Forest), Andy Gray (Aston Villa), Asa Hartford (Manchester City), and Arthur Graham (Leeds United).

SUNDAY 25TH OCTOBER 1998

The great and good of Scottish football gathered in Glasgow to celebrate the 125th anniversary of the Scottish Football Association. Luminaries from other countries were also invited to a lavish dinner and reception.

SATURDAY 26TH OCTOBER 1929

After the excitement of the summer tour earlier in the year when Scotland had taken on 'foreign' countries for the first time, old habits resumed with the start of the 1930 British Home Championship. Scotland made a winning start even if there was a fright en route to the points. A double from Hughie Gallacher ensured a half-time lead against Wales but after the restart two goals were immediately conceded to level the tie. Scotland eventually claimed the victory thanks to late strikes by Alex James and James Gibson.

SATURDAY 27TH OCTOBER 1928

Hughie Gallacher scored many important goals in his career but one of note was Scotland's 400th goal which came in the 1928 clash with Wales in the British Home Championship. Scotland came out on top 4-2, largely thanks to a hat-trick from Hughie which included the landmark strike. James Dunn scored the last Scottish goal of the day as Scotland made a winning start to the tournament. England and Scotland would both defeat Ireland and Wales to set up a winner-takes-all meeting at Hampden later in the season in which Scotland would triumph.

WEDNESDAY 28TH OCTOBER 2009

Young Islam Feruz fell under the spotlight of the media as he prepared to make his international debut for Scotland the next day. Though simply a talented teenager, Islam was also about to become the first player to represent Scotland despite not being born in the country or having relatives who were. He had arrived as a refugee from Somalia in the 1990s and was about to benefit from a new ruling proposed by SFA chief executive Gordon Smith, and agreed by the other Home Nations, which would allow players to be capped if they had a British passport and had been educated in their country of choice for five years. This helped move Scotland closer into line with the selection policies of other countries and should allow the multicultural nature of modern Scottish society to be represented in the national team. Islam had a debut to remember as he scored the only goal in Scotland under-16s' win over their Welsh counterparts.

TUESDAY 29TH OCTOBER 1975

After defeating Denmark in Copenhagen at the start of the qualification campaign for the 1976 European Championship, the Scotland side created problems with the resulting celebratory night out. The behaviour in the city centre and, perhaps even more significantly, back at the hotel afterwards, had led to life bans being handed to five players, though two would later be recalled. This ensured it was a changed Scottish side which lined up for the return match with the Danes at Hampden but the outcome would be the same. Kenny Dalglish, Bruce Rioch and Ted MacDougall scored the goals as Scotland won 3-1.

WEDNESDAY 30TH OCTOBER 1974

Around 15 years since their compatriots from the West visited Scotland, East Germany arrived at Hampden for the first time in 1974. Though overshadowed by West Germany winning the World Cup a few months previously, East Germany had also enjoyed a very credible tournament and even defeated the eventual champions in one of the earlier rounds. They were no match for the Scots on this occasion as goals from Tommy Hutchison, Kenny Burns and Kenny Dalglish secured victory. Scotland played East Germany six times during the country's relatively short period of existence, winning two, drawing one and losing three of the encounters.

SATURDAY 31ST OCTOBER 1903

Hampden Park opened in its present location on this day as Queen's Park defeated Celtic 1-0. The ground has a long history which dates back well beyond the current site in Glasgow's Mount Florida as the current Hampden Park is actually the third stadium of that name! Scotland's football pioneers, Queen's Park, initially played at a stadium named Hampden but moved to a new ground, also called Hampden, in 1884. They played there for several years but, confident in the future of the game and sensing the need for expansion, sold this ground to Third Lanark and moved to the present site in the south side of Glasgow. Thirds renamed their new ground Cathkin Park and though the club went out of business in the 1960s, the remnants of the huge swathes of concrete terracing can still be seen around the football field which now hosts amateur games. Queen's Park spared no expense in constructing the third Hampden and when they played their first match at the ground it really was a stadium for the 20th century, believed to be the biggest and most technically advanced in the world. Scotland would not make Hampden their permanent home until much later but it was soon apparent that for the big games against England, Hampden – whose capacity dwarfed that of Ibrox and Celtic Park – was the only option. It has since been dusted down many times before complete redevelopment in the 1990s turned it into the modern all-seater venue it is today. Those who stood on the never-ending terraces must wonder just how the home of Scottish football can get by with a capacity of 'only' 52,000!

SCOTLAND
On This Day

NOVEMBER

MONDAY 1st NOVEMBER 2004

Berti Vogts paid the price for the poor form of his Scotland team when he was sacked from his position on this day. His harshest critics laid several charges against him which went all the way back to his first games in charge – a 5-0 friendly humiliation against France and, arguably even worse, drawing in the Faroe Islands. The 6-0 debacle in Holland had been followed by some utterly abject friendly performances against Wales and Hungary before a disastrous start to the 2006 World Cup qualifying group brought only draws against Slovenia and Moldova and a loss at home to Norway. In defence of Vogts, he simply did not have many experienced players capable of playing at international level and his willingness to blood youngsters such as Craig Gordon, Darren Fletcher and James McFadden helped lay the foundations for future managers.

MONDAY 2nd NOVEMBER 1970

Manager Bobby Brown was in confident mood going into the start of the qualifying group for the 1972 European Championships. He was reported as saying the squad he named for the Denmark clash at Hampden Park was "covered for any eventuality".

THURSDAY 3rd NOVEMBER 1960

After the departure of Andy Beattie, Ian McColl was next to be appointed to the hot seat of Scottish manager. He would spend five years in charge of the team and enjoyed triumphs in both 1962 and 1963 when Scotland won the British Home Championship outright. Unfortunately, despite several wins, the 1962 World Cup qualifying campaign was an ace short of success as it ended with a play-off loss to eventual runners-up Czechoslovakia. He left his position in 1965 to take over as manager of Sunderland.

THURSDAY 3rd NOVEMBER 1994

John Spencer scored one of the best goals in European competition when he ran the length of the park to score an away goal against Austria Vienna for Chelsea in the Cup Winners' Cup. However, despite his obvious talent he failed to score once for Scotland in 14 caps although he did play in all three games in the finals of Euro 96 in England.

WEDNESDAY 4TH NOVEMBER 1953

Scotland were held to a 3-3 draw at home to Wales and missed the chance to secure qualification to the World Cup finals of 1954. Having already defeated Northern Ireland in Belfast, another victory here would have guaranteed a place in the top two of the 1954 British Home Championship. This was being used as a qualifying group for the finals in Switzerland. However, though the draw kept Wales' dreams alive in the short term, they lost to Northern Ireland in their next game meaning Scotland qualified before they played again.

THURSDAY 4TH NOVEMBER 2004

The SFA were left looking for a short-term solution to fill the manager's post having sacked Berti Vogts and they appointed assistant Tommy Burns as caretaker boss. Burns' main task was to prepare a squad for the friendly against Sweden later in the month but his chances of getting the job on a permanent basis faltered at Easter Road. James McFadden's late penalty was scant consolation in a dismal 4-1 defeat.

WEDNESDAY 5TH NOVEMBER 1958

Even though Scotland took on Northern Ireland on a Wednesday afternoon, there was still a very healthy attendance at Hampden Park. They witnessed a scoreless first half but Dave Herd and Bobby Collins put Scotland two goals to the good after the break and the side seemed in complete control. Things changed when Eric Caldow scored an own goal and the Irish successfully swarmed forward in chase of an equaliser. Scotland were eventually lucky to start the 1959 British Home Championship with a point.

WEDNESDAY 6TH NOVEMBER 1957

Scotland guaranteed qualification for the 1958 World Cup in Sweden with a 3-2 win over Switzerland. The Swiss had already been defeated by the Scots in Basel at the beginning of the campaign but they had taken a point from their trip to Spain meaning Scotland held the advantage in the group despite a win and a loss of their own against the Spanish. Spain still had one more game to play but that was rendered meaningless as Scotland, despite some late edgy moments, held their nerve to progress.

WEDNESDAY 7TH NOVEMBER 1962

Denis Law joined the elite group of Scottish players to have scored four goals in a single game when he inspired Scotland to victory against Northern Ireland in this British Home Championship clash. Willie Henderson scored the other goal in a 5-1 victory as Scotland took an impressive step on the path to retaining the title they had won outright earlier in the year.

THURSDAY 7TH NOVEMBER 1963

Exactly a year to the day Denis Law scored four against Northern Ireland, he scored four against Norway. This made him the only player to have achieved the feat twice for Scotland. The goals came in a 6-1 demolition of the hapless Norwegians in a friendly match at Hampden Park. Dave Mackay scored the other goals and for once could finally celebrate finding the net; his only other Scotland goals had come in very heavy defeats, 4-1 against Austria in 1960 and in the 9-3 disaster against England at Wembley in 1961.

WEDNESDAY 8TH NOVEMBER 1961

Ian St John was in the middle of a hot streak for Scotland as he bagged a brace to secure a Home Championship win over Wales. The striker was in a spell when he would find the net five times in just four games for Scotland as he was on a high following his big-money move to Liverpool from Motherwell. At Fir Park he had established himself as one of the best of Bobby Ancell's young side and made headlines north and south of the border with a sensational hat-trick against Hibs which took only two-and-a-half minutes from start to finish. A hat-trick was the perfect way to start his Liverpool career and he went on to be a huge success at the Anfield club, winning the league and scoring the winner in the 1965 FA Cup Final. His Scottish career ended with 21 caps and nine international goals and he moved into management with Motherwell and Portsmouth. In the 1980s he was also famous for combining with Jimmy Greaves in a television football show whereby playing the straight man, he managed to make his fair share of digs and jokes at the expense of his partner.

WEDNESDAY 9TH NOVEMBER 1960

Jim Baxter made the first of his 34 international appearances for Scotland in a British Home Championship game against Northern Ireland. He made a winning start as goals from Denis Law, Eric Caldow, George Young and a Ralph Brand double secured an entertaining 5-2 victory.

TUESDAY 9TH NOVEMBER 1965

Italian newspaper *Guerin Sportivo* led with the headline "Beasts of Glasgow" and a partisan article suggested that Italy had always been hated in Scotland. Quite what brought about this allegation is unclear but the newspaper may have felt justified with the 'beasts' label as a heaving Hampden Park roared Scotland to a famous victory against Italy. Over 100,000 people were in the ground to watch Scotland battle bravely for 90 minutes and then steal the points at the death. Defender John Greig pushed forward late on and when the ball returned to his path after a neat one-two, he swept a low shot into the net to keep Scotland's dream alive of qualifying for the World Cup finals in England – at least until the return match in Naples.

WEDNESDAY 10TH NOVEMBER 1971

Kenny Dalglish won the first of his 102 caps against Belgium in a European Championship qualifier played in Aberdeen. A crowd of nearly 37,000 watched the man who would go on to be Scotland's most capped player don the dark blue for the first time and they went home happy as John O'Hare scored in a 1-0 win.

SUNDAY 10TH NOVEMBER 1996

Jim Leighton produced one of the finest individual performances ever seen for Scotland as Sweden were defeated 1-0 at Ibrox. The continuing redevelopment of Hampden caused Scotland to take to grounds around the country as they looked to qualify for France 98 but this important tie was played in front of a large Ibrox crowd. John McGinlay opened the scoring but the Swedes were soon well on top. Particularly in the second half they seemed to cut through the home defence at will but save after save by Leighton kept them out and Scotland somehow managed to hold on to claim the three points.

WEDNESDAY 11TH NOVEMBER 1987

Scotland's competitive interest in the 1988 European Championships had already ended when they travelled to Bulgaria for the final game but the hosts needed a result to secure their own place at the finals. However, Gary Mackay scored the only goal of the game on his debut to send the Bulgarians crashing out and allow the Republic of Ireland to travel to West Germany in their place. The Irish showed their gratitude in typical fashion by sending Mackay a crate of Irish whiskey while the SFA received champagne – though one hopes that was imported and not a national product!

WEDNESDAY 12TH NOVEMBER 1986

Kenny Dalglish played his last match for Scotland in a comfortable 3-0 win against Luxembourg at Hampden. Dalglish, two years previously, had equalled the Scottish scoring record held by Denis Law with a sensational goal against Spain but he could not find the extra strike he needed in his final six appearances to take sole possession of the honour.

WEDNESDAY 12TH NOVEMBER 1997

Craig Brown started Scotland's preparation for the 1998 World Cup finals with a tough trip to take on hosts France in a November friendly. Gordon Durie scored an equaliser just 60 seconds after France opened the scoring but the French would emerge victorious in St Etienne through a late penalty. Scotland would return to the city for the third group game in the World Cup finals, needing a win against Morocco.

SATURDAY 12TH NOVEMBER 2005

When Scotland first took on the USA in 1952 at Hampden, the hosts cruised to a comfortable 6-0 win. The Americans improved over time, though, and this remains the only occasion when Scotland have come out on top in a full encounter between the sides. The Americans had won two out of three, with the other being drawn, in the 1990s, before the last game to date between the countries was played in November 2005. An early penalty gave the USA the lead at Hampden but Andy Webster headed home to secure a draw although Scott Brown, on his debut, had a late winner disallowed.

SATURDAY 13TH NOVEMBER 1999

Hampden Park was rocking as England visited for the first time in ten years as the historic rivals met in the first leg of a play-off to reach the finals of Euro 2000. Scotland played well in places but were missing a crucial component of the side as Paul Lambert had been injured in a recent Old Firm derby. In the absence of Scotland's midfield blocker, Paul Scholes twice ghosted through to score goals although had Kevin Gallacher's effort which struck the bar dropped into the net to level the game things could have been different. Scotland would head to Wembley needing a minor miracle to turn the situation around and progress to the finals.

WEDNESDAY 14TH NOVEMBER 1934

Dave Mackay, one of Scotland's most successful football exports, was born in Edinburgh on this day. He started off his career with a successful spell at Hearts which included a Scottish championship and multiple League Cup triumphs before he moved to Spurs. International recognition had already come his way at Tynecastle but at White Hart Lane he played a crucial role in making the club one of the best in the country; double winners and kings of Europe as they won the Cup Winners' Cup. He played against France in the 1958 World Cup finals and though success was harder to come by with the national team he tasted both victory and defeat against England before ending his Scottish career with 22 caps.

WEDNESDAY 14TH NOVEMBER 1973

West Germany visited Scotland for a friendly in Glasgow but the game almost fell victim to a ban on floodlights during the three-day week. This midweek clash finished hours before the axe fell on evening fixtures and Jim Holton's goal secured a 1-1 draw against the visitors.

WEDNESDAY 14TH NOVEMBER 1984

Denis Law's scoring record of 30 goals lasted only 12 years. Kenny Dalglish scored a sensational third goal against Spain, cutting along the box before shooting high into the top corner, to ensure Scotland claimed a 3-1 win in this qualifying clash for the 1986 World Cup.

MONDAY 15TH NOVEMBER 1971

The early 1970s were testing times for Hampden as the famous ground was in urgent need of repair but few people seemed willing or able to put up the necessary cash. There was a boost for fans of the stadium on this day, however, as the SFA council voted to retain Hampden as the home of the national team for the foreseeable future.

WEDNESDAY 15TH NOVEMBER 2000

Willie Cunningham, Scotland's first captain at the World Cup finals, died on this day. Born in Fife, he had initially made his living in the pits but his talent for football soon shone through and saw him move to Preston North End following spells at Dunfermline and Airdrie. For Scotland he had entered the side in the build-up to the finals of 1954 and was captain in both of the matches against Austria and Uruguay. The anecdotes about the SFA's preparation for the tournament are numerous but one which left Cunningham embarrassed was that he had no pennant to exchange with his Austrian counterpart in the first tie.

SATURDAY 15TH NOVEMBER 2003

The high point of the Berti Vogts era came at a drizzly Hampden Park when Scotland defeated Holland 1-0 in the Euro 2004 play-off first leg. Scotland enjoyed their share of luck as the Dutch went close to scoring on numerous occasions and also had a strong penalty appeal turned down. The only goal was scored by James McFadden as he cut inside following a delightful flick from Darren Fletcher to give the Scots hope of causing a dramatic upset going into the return leg in Amsterdam.

MONDAY 16TH NOVEMBER 2009

The SFA bowed to the inevitable and sacked George Burley. The manager had presided over a disastrous World Cup qualifying campaign which saw Scotland knocked out of play-off contention by Norway as Holland won the group. Improved performances in the final two games caused the SFA to give Burley two autumn friendly matches to prove he was finally on the right track but a loss to Japan and humiliation in Wales left their hands tied.

WEDNESDAY 17th NOVEMBER 1948

A Billy Houliston double and a strike from Jimmy Mason earned a 3-2 victory against Northern Ireland after Scotland had trailed by two goals. It is the last comeback of this kind up to September 1st 2010.

WEDNESDAY 17th NOVEMBER 1993

After the departure of Andy Roxburgh from the position of national coach, the SFA made an internal promotion by appointing assistant manager Craig Brown as his successor. His immediate goal was to build a side capable of qualifying for Euro 96 and he achieved that and reached the World Cup finals in France 98, before narrowly missing out on Euro 2000 in a play-off with England. His spell ended in failing to reach the 2002 World Cup and Brown resigned before going on to manage Preston North End and Motherwell.

WEDNESDAY 17th NOVEMBER 1999

Scotland had a mountain to climb as they tried to overcome a 2-0 deficit at Wembley to reach Euro 2000. Craig Brown's side played with skill and belief and Don Hutchison's header before half-time encouraged hope of a miracle. Scotland pressed but clear chances were rare and David Seaman's point-blank save from Christian Dailly saw the English squeak home. Scotland took minor consolation in winning the last Auld Enemy clash at the old Wembley before it was torn down.

SATURDAY 17th NOVEMBER 2007

"The day a nation has been waiting for" was how commentator Paul Mitchell introduced the match with Italy which could have seen Scotland reach Euro 2008 with a victory, exit with a loss or be left waiting with a draw. A terrible start saw Luca Toni open the scoring within seconds and Antonio Di Natale had another disallowed as Scotland struggled with nerves. Gradually things changed and Barry Ferguson's scrambled equaliser set up a dramatic final third. Scotland looked set for the win as James McFadden slid in at the back post but at full stretch he could not direct his shot on target with Buffon beaten. The last hope vanished in the final minute when Christian Panucci headed home a soft free kick to break Scottish hearts again.

DON HUTCHISON SCORED A NUMBER OF IMPORTANT GOALS FOR SCOTLAND.

WEDNESDAY 18TH NOVEMBER 1981

The World Cup qualification campaign of 1982 ended with a dead rubber in Lisbon but on this occasion it was Scotland who were looking forward to the finals while Portugal prepared to stay home. The Portuguese regained some pride by winning this game 2-1 as the Scots went down despite a goal by Paul Sturrock.

SATURDAY 19TH NOVEMBER 2003

Scotland's Euro 2004 qualification dreams were shattered on the floor of the Amsterdam Arena as Holland romped to a 6-0 win. Though defending a single goal lead from the first leg of the play-off, Scotland were outclassed from start to finish and rarely threatened to find the result they needed. Without the suspended Christian Dailly sitting in front of the back four to break up play, the hosts strolled through the midfield at will and the Scottish cause was further hampered by some shambolic defending. The score was 3-0 at half-time, six by the end and were it not for Dutch mercy, could have been even higher.

WEDNESDAY 20TH NOVEMBER 1985

Australia visited Hampden for the first leg of the play-off to reach the World Cup finals in Mexico but despite turning in a determined display, they were eventually beaten 2-0. Scotland needed a long time to make the breakthrough but it finally arrived when Davie Cooper lashed a powerful free kick low into the bottom corner. Moments later Frank McAvennie beat the advancing goalkeeper to the ball to give Scotland a healthy advantage going into the return match in Melbourne in early December.

WEDNESDAY 20TH NOVEMBER 1991

Scotland were left with a nervous wait as the qualification campaign for Euro 92 came to an end. A 4-0 win over San Marino in the final game meant Scotland would progress to the finals if Romania failed to win in Sofia by two clear goals. The tension was increased as the Romanians took a first-half lead through Gheorghe Popescu but an equaliser by Nasko Sirakov after the break allowed the Scots to celebrate as they reached the final stages of this competition for the first time.

TUESDAY 21st NOVEMBER 1950

Tommy Craig was the first Scottish player transferred to an English club for a six-figure fee. Craig was born in Penilee on this day. He had made a big impact after breaking through at Aberdeen and was not yet out of his teens when Sheffield Wednesday brought him to Hillsborough. His fine performances south of the border brought him into the Scotland international set-up and he was made captain of both the under-21 and under-23 sides. However, despite this endorsement he did not quite make the progress that was hoped of him and he was capped only once, against Switzerland, in 1976.

WEDNESDAY 21st NOVEMBER 1956

George Young became the first Scottish player to reach the 50-cap landmark when he captained the side to a 2-0 friendly victory against Yugoslavia. Young was the most capped player for a spell and eventually finished his career on 53 international appearances although he was suddenly dropped from the Scotland team midway through the qualification campaign for the 1958 World Cup.

SUNDAY 22nd NOVEMBER 1959

Scottish football icon Frank McAvennie was born. Though he scored only one goal in the dark blue of Scotland, it was a vital strike as it came against Australia in the play-off for the 1986 World Cup finals. McAvennie was a clinical striker and scored notable goals for both Celtic and West Ham after coming through the ranks at St Mirren. His off-field antics soon became well known as he developed a taste for the high life and the Scottish football parody programme, *Only an Excuse*, made him a popular and recurring character.

WEDNESDAY 23rd NOVEMBER 1966

Kevin Gallacher was born on this day in Clydebank. Gallacher played 53 times in total for Scotland, scoring nine goals, with the majority of these coming in a purple patch when qualifying for the World Cup in 1998. Gallacher grabbed six goals as Scotland reached the finals in France and though he failed to find the net at the World Cup itself, he did play in all three games.

WEDNESDAY 24th NOVEMBER 1965

Scotland recovered from a loss in their opening game in the 1966 British Home Championship to thrash Wales 4-1 at Hampden Park. A double from Bobby Murdoch and goals from Willie Henderson and John Greig secured victory but this proved to be the lone high point of the campaign as Scotland also lost the final game at home to England.

TUESDAY 25th NOVEMBER 1959

Future Scotland player Jim Bett was born in Hamilton on this day in 1959. He endured a low-key start to his playing career in his native country before moving to Valur in Iceland. From there his next stop was Belgium and it was with Lokeren that he really made his name. A move to Rangers followed, and the first of his 25 international caps, before he returned to Belgium and Lokeren once more. He then moved to Aberdeen, where his subtle passing and skilful play helped win the Scottish Cup in 1986 and 1989. Ironically, his only international goal came in one of the countries where he had played league football as he netted a late winner against Iceland.

SUNDAY 25th NOVEMBER 2007

The eyes of the world turned to South Africa as the qualifying groups were drawn for the 2010 World Cup. Scotland were on a high despite missing out on the finals of the European Championship earlier in the month and their performances in that campaign had earned them a place among the second seeds for this tournament. Scotland were placed in group I, which contained only five teams, and while top seeds Holland were strong favourites to top the table, there was confidence that Iceland, Macedonia and Norway could be handled and the play-offs would be reached once again.

SATURDAY 26th NOVEMBER 1983

There seemed to be no end in sight for the scoring prowess of Kenny Dalglish. The King of the Kop scored his 100th league goal for Liverpool on this day against Ipswich Town and having already achieved that feat with Celtic, became the first player to reach this tally both north and south of the border.

TUESDAY 27TH NOVEMBER 2007

Alex McLeish decided against leading Scotland into the 2010 World Cup qualifying campaign and left his post as manager to take over at Birmingham City. McLeish had taken the job midway through the previous campaign but had made a fantastic impression by taking the team to within a couple of points of the Euro 2008 finals. His record of seven wins from ten games was exceptional but once more Scotland would have to look for a new boss, their fifth of the decade.

MONDAY 28TH NOVEMBER 1938

Scotland goalkeeper Frank Haffey was born in Glasgow. He would become infamous for being between the posts in the 9-3 disaster against England in 1961, his second cap after also playing England the previous year. He was never picked for Scotland again. It is rare to absolve the goalkeeper from blame when nine goals have been conceded but Haffey was one of the scapegoats for what had been a collectively poor performance. It has been reported that he was singing in the bath after the game at Wembley and Denis Law commented that for a goalkeeper he was a good singer!

WEDNESDAY 29TH NOVEMBER 1933

When Scotland drew 2-2 with Austria at Hampden Park, there were three countries represented on the pitch. Goalkeeper Joe Kennaway won his only Scottish cap in this game but he had previously been honoured by Canada as he had also played international 'soccer' for them in a match against the USA.

WEDNESDAY 29TH NOVEMBER 1961

Scotland and Czechoslovakia had finished deadlocked in the qualifying group for the 1962 World Cup so a play-off was arranged in Brussels to see who would take a place at the finals which were to be hosted in Chile. Scotland fought bravely against a quality side and even led twice through goals from Ian St John. However, it was not to be as the Czechs managed to step up their performance to score a late equaliser and found two more goals in extra time to win the contest 4-2. They would eventually finish runners-up to Brazil in Chile.

SATURDAY 30TH NOVEMBER 1872

The first official international football match was played between Scotland and England on St Andrew's Day 1872. The game in Glasgow, which was played at the West of Scotland's cricket ground in Partick, finished 0-0, although Scotland did seem to go closer to the winning goal. Reports vary of just how hard done by they were not to emerge with a historic first victory. The Scottish team was provided entirely by Queen's Park, the leading Scottish club of the day, and even Queen's Park kits were used by the Scots rather than unique shirts. Up to September 2010, the Scotland–England fixture has been contested 110 times with Scotland winning 41 and drawing 24, while England have enjoyed 45 triumphs.

THURSDAY 30TH NOVEMBER 1944

George Graham was born on this day in Coatbridge. As a player he was best known for his time at Arsenal where he won the Fairs Cup and made an important contribution to the side which won the double in 1971. He picked up 12 Scotland caps, scoring three goals, in the first half of the 1970s but he had dropped out of contention from the national pool before the World Cup of 1974. After serving his managerial apprenticeship in the lower leagues, he became highly successful with Arsenal before being forced to resign in a bung scandal. He eventually returned to football but although linked with the Scotland post on a number of occasions the SFA declined to give him the chance to lead the team.

TUESDAY 30TH NOVEMBER 2004

Patience had been a virtue for Scottish goalkeeper Bill Brown who died on this day. He had been placed on stand-by to play for the national team no fewer than 24 times before finally making his debut in the World Cup finals when he was between the posts for the 2-1 defeat to France in 1958. He would establish himself as the number one over the next few years and earned the last of his 28 caps in the famous 1-0 victory over Italy at Hampden in 1965. His final number of appearances could have been even higher had his club, Spurs, not forbidden him from taking part in Scotland's European tours!

SCOTLAND
On This Day

DECEMBER

WEDNESDAY 1ST DECEMBER 1971

Scotland had made a strong finish to 1971 with a couple of wins to end the qualifying campaign for the 1972 European Championships but lost their final match of the year to Holland in Amsterdam. A George Graham equaliser was not enough to secure a draw as a goal from Barry Hulshoff just two minutes from time was enough to give the hosts a 2-1 friendly win. This was Graham's first strike for his country and he would also find the net twice against Wales in the British Home Championship to end his Scotland career with three goals in 12 appearances. The great Johan Cruyff had opened the scoring for Holland after only five minutes of the game while future Dutch World Cup finalists Ruud Krol, Wim Jansen, Johan Neeskens and Willem van Hanegem also featured in a strong Holland line-up.

WEDNESDAY 2ND DECEMBER 1987

Though Luxembourg has a long history of international football, to date they have played Scotland only three times. The first meeting resulted in a heavy Scotland victory in a friendly and the Scots also won the first competitive meeting between the sides. However, on the third meeting, at the end of the qualifying campaign for the 1988 European Championships, the small country held Scotland to a 0-0 draw at home to claim what was then a very rare point in international football. Luxembourg have improved since this day in 1987 but this result against a side containing players such as Mo Johnston, Paul McStay and Pat Nevin remains one of their best.

THURSDAY 2ND DECEMBER 2004

Scotland's hopes of reaching the World Cup in 2006 were hanging by a thread after draws against Moldova and Slovenia, and a loss against Norway, when Walter Smith was appointed manager on this day. His first game, away to Italy, was lost but he managed to restore respectability to the side even if qualification proved impossible. The Kirin Cup was won in the summer of 2006 but after leading the side to three wins in the first four games of an extremely difficult Euro 2008 qualifying group, he quit his post to return to Rangers as manager, a position he held from 1991 to 1998.

THURSDAY 3RD DECEMBER 1964

Tosh McKinlay was born on this day in Glasgow. He made steady progress throughout his career which started at Dundee before he moved to Hearts and then on to boyhood heroes Celtic. It was with the Parkhead club that he tasted success for the first time, winning the Scottish Cup in 1995 and earning his first full international cap to go with the honours he had won at under-21 and B level. Part of the squad which went to the World Cup finals in 1998, he featured in the group games against Brazil and Morocco.

THURSDAY 4TH DECEMBER 1958

Matt Busby resigned his position as Scotland manager on this day. The Munich air crash earlier in the year had meant he missed the World Cup in Sweden as he recovered over several months and he eventually began his duties in autumn, taking the side for two games. However, he was still not fully recovered and, following medical advice, decided to resign his position. Both parties indicated there could be a return some time in the future.

WEDNESDAY 4TH DECEMBER 1985

Scotland reached the World Cup finals in Mexico thanks to a 0-0 draw in Melbourne against Australia. The side were defending a two-goal lead from the first leg and while that offered some insurance, it was certainly not enough to take progression for granted. Goalkeeper Jim Leighton had an inspired game and he made a number of strong saves to ensure there was no way back for the Aussies. Scotland could start planning for their fourth World Cup finals in succession.

THURSDAY 5TH DECEMBER 1963

An inquest was held following Scotland under-23s losing 3-1 to Wales at Wrexham's Racecourse Ground the previous night, and largely featured on whether the selectors should change the policy of not selecting any player already holding a full international cap. This was prompted by a team of inexperienced youngsters being outclassed by a Welsh team that included four full internationals. It was suggested that Denis Law, Billy McNeill or Willie Henderson would have supplied inspiration and encouragement.

WEDNESDAY 6TH DECEMBER 1882

A decisive step was taken towards developing the game of football on this day in Manchester. The four home associations met to agree one set of rules for the sport which would later be accepted all over the world when other countries began to participate in internationals and develop their own domestic leagues.

MONDAY 6TH DECEMBER 1965

Striker Gordon Durie was born on this day. While his scoring record of seven goals in 43 internationals was not prolific, he played an important role in the squad throughout the 1980s and 90s. He was not at the top of the queue at the World Cup in 1990 but made one appearance against Sweden and played two games in the finals of Euro 92. By the time Scotland next reached a major finals in 1996 he was well established in the team and played in all three matches. He was unlucky not to score against England and won a penalty in that game. He also played in every game of the World Cup finals in 1998 having scored one of the goals against Latvia which ensured Scotland would travel to France.

TUESDAY 7TH DECEMBER 1965

Scotland made the journey to Italy in hope of securing the point which would take them to the 1966 World Cup finals. The Italians elected to play in the intimidating venue at Naples but manager Jock Stein was more concerned by the long list of players he had unavailable for selection. With few of his first-choice squad at his disposal there was little alternative but to hope for the best. The hope was a forlorn one though and Italy easily cruised to a 3-0 win meaning the Scots were excluded from the world championship taking place south of their border.

MONDAY 7TH DECEMBER 1970

Preparations for the next game at Wembley were underway at the SFA offices and those wanting to apply for tickets by postcard had until this day to do so. Perhaps those unlucky in their attempt were actually better off as Scotland would lose the contest 3-1.

SUNDAY 8TH DECEMBER 1963

Brian McClair was born in Bellshill in 1963. He first succeeded at Motherwell but really made his name north of the border as a prolific scorer with Celtic. After moving to Manchester United he continued to find the net regularly even if he began playing in a slightly deeper role. Despite his instinct for goal he needed 26 caps to open his account for Scotland and eventually finished with two goals in 30 appearances.

WEDNESDAY 8TH DECEMBER 1965

The country was wallowing in misery having been knocked out of the World Cup in Naples the previous day. Following reports by employers of widespread absenteeism as workers stayed away to watch the afternoon game, the *Glasgow Herald* was outraged and claimed such behaviour damaged the reputation of Scottish labour.

SUNDAY 8TH DECEMBER 1991

Many football people insist you make your own luck in the game but fate can certainly play a part too. Andy Roxburgh must have felt the gods conspired against him on this day in 1991 when Scotland were drawn in a brutally tough qualifying group for the 1994 World Cup. Though Malta and Estonia expected to struggle, Portugal, Switzerland and Italy fancied their chances of reaching the finals and Scotland faced the possibility of missing out.

WEDNESDAY 9TH DECEMBER 1942

Future Scotland captain Billy Bremner was born on this day in 1942. The aggressive midfielder was a key component of the Leeds side which was so successful in the 1960s and 70s but it would be wrong to paint him simply as a hard tackler. He was also a fine passer and chipped in goals, although one of the most famous images is of him trudging off the field at Wembley, topless, having been sent off for fighting Kevin Keegan. He collected 54 Scotland caps, many as captain, and featured heavily in the 1974 World Cup finals. While not as successful as a manager, he remains a hero to the Elland Road faithful and there is a large statue in his honour outside the ground. He died from illness, aged 54, in 1997.

TUESDAY 10TH DECEMBER 1968

Manager Bobby Brown did not have problems to seek as Scotland prepared to take on Cyprus. The journey to the island by plane, via Greece, had been both long and bumpy and the pilot insisted the plane be checked in the Greek capital before he continued to fly, meaning the trip lasted 14 hours! Things did not immediately improve in Cyprus as the side took to the training field only to discover Cypriot players and staff sitting in the stands watching them. Eventually the boss focussed on getting the players used to the very hard pitch on which the game would be played.

WEDNESDAY 11TH DECEMBER 1968

Scotland's clash with Cyprus was actually the first time the two countries had ever met on the football field. After the difficulties involved in getting to the island and preparing, Scotland would have few further problems as they strolled to a comfortable 5-0 win. The return match in Glasgow was won by an even bigger margin, 8-0, but Cyprus would make reasonably quick progress on the football stage. When Scotland next met them, in the qualifiers for Italia 90, both games would be won only by the odd goal in five, and three, respectively.

THURSDAY 12TH DECEMBER 1996

After the success of the under-17 World Cup in 1989, Scotland would open its doors again to host the under-16 European Championships of 1998. The qualifying rounds kicked off on this day to see who would join hosts Scotland in the finals but sadly this competition did not capture the imagination in the way of its predecessor. Scotland going out early on probably did not help matters!

THURSDAY 12TH DECEMBER 2002

After a spell of relatively poor results on the park, Scotland also tasted defeat in the campaign to host Euro 2008. Austria and Switzerland were awarded the tournament on this day but in truth the result was no surprise. After considering a solo bid, the Irish were belatedly added as partners and an overreliance on Glasgow – which was to provide three stadiums – meant Uefa were always likely to look elsewhere.

WEDNESDAY 13TH DECEMBER 1950

Creaking empires often fail to realise their time has passed before it is too late but there are usually warning signs on the way to ruin. A team from beyond the British Isles defeated Scotland at Hampden for the first time in 1950 when Austria triumphed 1-0 and just to prove it was no fluke, they dismantled Scotland in methodical fashion to record a 4-0 victory in Vienna a few months later.

SUNDAY 13TH DECEMBER 1970

Eoin Jess was born in Aberdeen on this day. A player with superb technique, he often used his pace to good effect by breaking from deep positions. He impressed at Aberdeen and earned a big-money move to Coventry City. Somewhere along the line things went slightly wrong though and while he did regain his form after returning to Aberdeen, his final total of two goals in 18 Scotland appearances is a little disappointing for a player who seemed to have the game at his feet as a youngster.

SATURDAY 14TH DECEMBER 1946

World Cup player Peter Lorimer was born on this day in Dundee. Don Revie won the race to sign him as a youngster and he was a crucial part of the Leeds team that was so successful in the late 1960s and early 1970s. He boasted a rocket shot but despite scoring regularly for his club, he managed only four goals in 21 appearances for Scotland. One of these goals took place on the biggest stage of all as he volleyed home a superb opener in Dortmund against Zaire in the 1974 World Cup finals.

SUNDAY 15TH DECEMBER 1985

The Hotel Chapultepac in Mexico City was the venue as the World Cup groups were drawn for the tournament the following year. Scotland had gone close to reaching the second round in the previous three competitions but were knocked out on goal difference each time. Their chances of progressing on this occasion were not helped by being drawn alongside West Germany, finalists in 1982, Denmark and Uruguay in what looked like a very tough group.

SUNDAY 16TH DECEMBER 1956

Former Scotland player and manager Tommy Burns was born on this day. Burns played at Celtic for 14 years and won several honours during this time. Despite being such a successful player with the Old Firm, he managed to collect only eight Scotland caps and travelled to neither the World Cup finals of 1982 or 1986. His commitment to the Scottish cause was seen after his playing days finished when he was appointed assistant manager to Berti Vogts and then employed as caretaker boss for a month when the German was dismissed. Burns hoped to secure the post in his own right but remained as assistant to Walter Smith who was offered the job. He was overlooked again when Smith rejoined Rangers in 2006 and then left the SFA.

WEDNESDAY 17TH DECEMBER 1919

Henry Morris, the only player to score a hat-trick on his Scotland debut and not be picked again, was born in Dundee in 1919. The striker had a simply outstanding scoring record in domestic football, with 154 goals in 177 games for East Fife, and appeared to make the most of his chance for Scotland when he scored three goals in the 8-2 thrashing of Northern Ireland in 1949. This was an era of several top quality strikers and despite this performance he was never given the opportunity to shine again. He left Bayview having won two League Cups and played with Dundee United and Portadown before retiring from football. He died, aged 73, in 1993.

WEDNESDAY 17TH DECEMBER 1975

Scotland ended the qualification campaign for the European Championships of 1976 with a 1-1 draw at home to Romania. Scotland lost only one game in the qualification group, at home to Spain, having drawn in Valencia. Despite beating Denmark home and away, points dropped to Romania in both games proved costly. Initially dwarfed by the World Cup, the European Championship was a small tournament and while Scotland often played well in their qualification group, they would often come up short in the face of one major football power. They reached the finals in the eight-team format just once, in 1992, and for the only other time to date in 1996.

TOMMY BURNS WAS A LONG-SERVING ASSISTANT MANAGER.

MONDAY 18TH DECEMBER 1972

Scotland received bad news from a Fifa meeting which decided to ban Peter Lorimer for two games following a red card against Denmark. The side had beaten Denmark, despite his dismissal, but the fate of the group would be decided in the two contests with Czechoslovakia which would take place without him in the autumn of 1973.

THURSDAY 18TH DECEMBER 1980

One of Scotland's finest strikers was born in Kilwinning in December. Julie Fleeting would become one of the leading players in the women's game, not just in Scotland but also in England and the USA before taking up a teaching post in Scotland. The Scottish women's team has not yet reached the level of other countries which have played for longer at the highest level but few players have done more to drag the team forward than Fleeting. A stunning record of 113 goals in 116 international games stands in comparison to any player in the world and after returning from the birth of her child she will hope to help Scotland reach the finals of a major tournament. Her efforts were recognised in 2008 when she was awarded the MBE for services to women's football.

SUNDAY 18TH DECEMBER 1994

Scotland's hopes of reaching the finals of Euro 96 in England took a blow when the side lost 1-0 to Greece in Athens. There was little between the teams, other than a first-half penalty, and Scotland were frustrated when their own spot kick appeal was turned down. However, this was the only loss of the campaign and Scotland would go on to qualify from the group.

THURSDAY 19TH DECEMBER 1946

Willie Johnston was born on this day in Glasgow in 1946. The controversial player was a talented winger who helped Rangers to the 1972 Cup Winners' Cup, but was cursed by a short temper and poor disciplinary record. He was sent home from the 1978 World Cup for failing a drug test after the loss to Peru and though he maintained this was an innocent mistake, the SFA had little sympathy for his defence.

MONDAY 20TH DECEMBER 1971

The SFA was considering its options for Scotland's first fixture of 1972. An offer from Rangers for a friendly match was eventually turned down but it was decided instead to line up a bounce game for the under-23 side against the West Germany Olympic team.

TUESDAY 21ST DECEMBER 1965

The SFA were preparing for a meeting with the other Home Nations the next day which would discuss participation in the 1968 European Championships. England had entered the competition in 1964, which was a knockout tournament, but the next version would adopt qualifying groups to reach a set of finals games similar to the World Cup. There were various possibilities to be considered including cutting back on the less glamorous British Home Championship fixtures while the SFA was concerned about the availability of England-based players to the national team. It was eventually decided to use the championship as qualifiers, like it was for the World Cups in 1950 and 1954.

SUNDAY 22ND DECEMBER 1963

The life of a back-up goalkeeper may be difficult but harder still is the hand dealt to a third choice keeper. Bryan Gunn was an excellent servant between the posts for Norwich City but he was competing for international caps against Jim Leighton and Andy Goram, two of the finest goalkeepers Scotland has ever produced. He eventually finished his career having played six times for Scotland and he also made a non-playing trip to the World Cup finals in 1990.

THURSDAY 22ND DECEMBER 1988

Scotland have never played later in any calendar year than in 1988 when they took on Italy in a friendly. The side had made a solid start to the qualifying campaign for the 1990 World Cup with a win over Norway and a draw against Yugoslavia but faced a crucial spring in 1989 with two games against Cyprus sandwiching a match with France. Although he made a couple of changes to the best eleven, manager Andy Roxburgh sent out a strong side for this contest in Perugia but went down 2-0 to the World Cup hosts.

SUNDAY 23rd DECEMBER 1979

Kenny Miller was born on this day in 1979. After making a big impact at Hibs, he moved to Rangers before joining Celtic after a spell down south. Not content at crossing the Old Firm divide once, he eventually went back to Rangers and has the rare distinction of scoring for both sides in Glasgow derby games. Internationally, he has sometimes struggled to find the net on a regular basis but he has been considered an important member of the squad by several managers who recognised his qualities and is well on course to reach the 50-cap mark.

WEDNESDAY 23rd DECEMBER 2009

After days of intense media speculation, Craig Levein was announced as the new Scotland manager at a Hampden press conference. He was offered the job ahead of several other candidates from both Scotland and further afield. He left his post at Dundee United to take over the national team and was charged with picking up the pieces following what had been a disastrous time under the leadership of George Burley. The qualifying draw for Euro 2012 grouped Scotland with defending champions Spain, the Czech Republic, Lithuania and Liechtenstein. His first game was a successful friendly against the Czechs and he threw himself into strengthening the available player pool by building bridges with some who had previously left the camp, and checking the eligibility of others through bloodlines.

TUESDAY 24th DECEMBER 1985

Former Scotland player Erich Schaedler committed suicide on this day in 1985. His father played for Borussia Mönchengladbach before becoming a prisoner of war and, ironically, Erich made his Scotland appearance against West Germany in 1974. Unfortunately, he suffered personal problems after football and took his life on this Christmas Eve.

TUESDAY 24th DECEMBER 1996

The Scotland team was also touched by tragedy in 1996. Bobby Robinson, who earned four Scottish caps in the mid-1970s, died on this day, aged only 46. He won his only major honour, the League Cup, with Dundee in 1974 but also helped Hearts win promotion back to the Premier League as First Division champions in 1980.

FRIDAY 25TH DECEMBER 1964

Future Scotland captain Gary McAllister was born in Motherwell in 1964. After breaking through at his local club he was transferred to Leicester City before he truly made his name with Leeds United. After a spell at Coventry City led to a move to Liverpool, he finished his career with a large haul of medals including the league championship in 1992 and the Uefa Cup in 2001 where he set up the winning goal. He played 57 times for Scotland, including at both Euro 92 and Euro 96, but missed the 1998 World Cup due to injury. Though his career ended on a sour note, when a minority of fans booed him in a game against the Czech Republic, he is remembered as one of the finest Scotland midfielders of recent times.

THURSDAY 26TH DECEMBER 2002

Young forward James McFadden showed his potential once more by scoring the winning goal for Motherwell against Rangers. McFadden had netted a winner against Celtic earlier in the season but despite his goals, Motherwell would finish bottom of the SPL in this season.

MONDAY 27TH DECEMBER 1971

Another one of Scotland's nearly men, Duncan Ferguson, was born on this day in 1971. He persuaded Rangers to pay Dundee United nearly £4m for his signature but after being jailed for an on-field headbutt – he had been in trouble with the law before – he was soon transferred to Everton. He became a cult hero in two spells at Goodison and won the FA Cup in 1995. He failed to recreate his form for Scotland and then withdrew himself from consideration for the team after playing seven times.

THURSDAY 28TH DECEMBER 1939

Frank McLintock was born in Glasgow. His senior football career began in England and he reached two FA Cup finals with Leicester City before moving to Arsenal. After a poor period for the club, he became a great captain of their double side in 1971 and following his Scotland debut in 1963 he went on to earn a total of nine caps, his last coming in a Wembley defeat of 1971.

TUESDAY 29th DECEMBER 2009

Former Scotland manager Craig Brown's coaching career went full circle when he returned to Motherwell. He had taken his first coaching job at Fir Park in the 1970s and showed he had not lost his touch by leading the team to European football.

SATURDAY 30th DECEMBER 1961

Charlie Nicholas was born on this day. After exploding through the ranks in a blizzard of goals at Celtic he moved to Arsenal. The London club struggled during his time at Highbury, although he did play a big role in the League Cup win of 1987. When he returned to Scotland, with Aberdeen, the best of his international career seemed behind him but he did finish with the respectable tally of five goals in 20 caps, including a stunning volley on his debut, plus appearances at the World Cup finals of 1986.

TUESDAY 31st DECEMBER 1941

Sir Alex Ferguson celebrates his birthday on Hogmanay. Born in Govan in 1941, he impressed with St Johnstone before earning a move to Rangers. His time at Ibrox was not completely successful and his playing career was unremarkable. He more than made up for it by becoming one of the best managers in the world, leading Aberdeen to success beyond their wildest dreams in the 1980s and taking Manchester United to the pinnacle of football, winning the Champions League twice, in 1998 and 2008. After the death of Jock Stein in 1985, he guided Scotland to the World Cup finals in Mexico but his impending move to Old Trafford ensured he left this post after the tournament.

FRIDAY 31st DECEMBER 1982

A mainstay of Scotland squads throughout recent campaigns, goalkeeper Craig Gordon was born on this day. After helping Hearts to win the Scottish Cup and reach the Champions League qualifiers, he moved to Sunderland for a fee which could eventually reach £10m, a record for any Scottish player. He was a vital component of the team during the Euro 2008 qualifiers, including both victories against France, but injury restricted his involvement in the attempt to reach the 2010 World Cup.

—